SELF FOR AT-RISK TEENS

OVERCOME THE ODDS AND LIVE THE LIFE OF YOUR DREAMS

BEN POVLOW

DEDICATION

To my wife, Kathi, and stepdaughter, Katelyn, thank you both for all your love, support, and encouragement. Your inspiration has helped me turn my ideas into a dream come true.

To all my family, my wife's family, all our friends, and our family cats, Tucker and Abby.

To you, the reader, thank you for purchasing this book. Please use this information to improve the quality of your life.

To all my family members, friends, and acquaintances who have passed away over the years. This book is dedicated to your memory. May you all rest in peace.

Thank you, God, for giving me the strength to write these words.

TABLE OF CONTENTS

INTRODUCTION

I was raised in unfortunate circumstances, but I believe the way I handled it made things much worse than they should have been. I now realize my life as a young adult had been the consequence of my poor decisions as a teenager. I was not prepared to become an adult. The main goal of this book is to teach you the things I wish I had known when I was your age—how to become independent, take care of yourself and avoid the dangerous pitfalls associated with being *at-risk*.

I have since changed my life for the better, but I can't change my past. What I can control is what I do with all the knowledge I've gained from my experiences. I will talk about what has worked for me and the areas of my life where I wish I would have done things differently. I am choosing to share this wisdom with you, so you can avoid making the same mistakes I made.

If I could go back and change my life, this book is what I would use as a guide. Throughout this book, you will learn a wide range of information that will help you get from where you are to where you want to go in your life. Everything I talk about in this book is based on personal experiences and self-taught knowledge. These are not things I learned in a traditional classroom. I am combining my street smarts and common sense, mixed with a wide range of practical life experiences, and proven self-help and personal development strategies to give you an education like no one else can.

The first time I picked up a self-help book, my life was changed forever. When I realized I could change the course of my life by changing what I was putting into my mind, it was game on. I turned off the radio and put on an audiobook. I turned off the TV and started reading inspirational books. It started with small changes, and before I knew it, I was hooked.

I started going to seminars of the most recognizable names in self-improvement. For several years I followed these leaders around the country, soaking up their knowledge and investing a lot of money into learning how to become the best version of myself I could be.

My journey of personal improvement started fourteen years ago. I began by changing my self-image and focusing on becoming a better person. I overcame my limiting beliefs and began to create a vision for my future. I went on to develop skills in leadership, team building, coaching, public speaking, sales, and how to make money on the internet. I became good enough to start conducting seminars and teaching others what I was learning.

If this is the first book you are reading on personal improvement, welcome to the journey of a lifetime. Self-discovery is one of the most exciting things you will ever experience. Once you realize what you're truly capable of, your life will never be the same. Strive to live up to your true potential. I know it's possible and I know you can do it.

Learning how to overcome the odds and create a better life for yourself is a choice anyone can make. The life skills and personal development strategies I'll be sharing will give you the knowledge you need to get from where you are now to where you want to go in life. I believe in you. Just by holding this book, you have already taken the first step. Congratulations!

CHAPTER 1

WHAT IS PUTTING YOU AT RISK?

L ife isn't always fair. We are all born into different circumstances. Why do some people have it better than others?
There is no one answer to this question. As a baby, we
don't have a choice about what our lives are like, but once we get
old enough to know what's going on, it's our job to take control
of our situation. Now is that time for you.

Growing up, I thought my circumstances were normal, and
everyone had the same situations going on in their lives. All my
friends came from broken homes; this was my reality. I was not
aware of how my life was different from other kids who were
being raised by two parents.

I never knew how good other families' lives were. As a kid, I got used to being told we couldn't afford the things I wanted. Growing up on welfare was no fun. We were getting powdered milk and government cheese as a handout and using food stamps to buy the other essentials. My mom worked, but apparently, it was still a struggle to raise two boys on her own.

Being raised by a single mother was all I ever knew. My parents separated when I was three years old and never got back together. My father was never around; I only remember meeting him one time when I was about ten, only months before he suddenly passed away.

I know my mom wasn't perfect, and I'm not sure why my parents couldn't make their marriage work. Unfortunately, I was never able to have an adult conversation with my mom because she passed away from cancer when I was sixteen. I wasn't prepared to handle this kind of loss. I did what I had to do to survive, but I made a lot of bad decisions in the process.

The term *at-risk* doesn't need to be a bad thing. It's only negative if you let it be. If you don't know you're at risk, you could suffer the consequences before you even know what has happened to you. If you understand up front that you are at risk, you can better prepare yourself for handling different situations when they show up.

If you don't know right from wrong, your behavior will reflect it. Looking back now, I can see the warning signs. They were all around me. I just didn't notice them because I wasn't paying attention. When you're a teenager, or even younger, your focus is on hanging out with your friends and having fun. Spending time with your family is usually the last thing on your mind.

The first big warning sign for me was that I resisted authority as a young child. It was in fifth grade when my behavior issues started to show, even though I didn't realize why. I was expelled from elementary school and forced to go to a new school in a different neighborhood with kids I didn't know.

After being expelled in the fifth grade, instead of trying to correct my behavior, I went on to have more and more issues over the next several years. Looking back on the situation, I realize now that had I known what my life would have become, I would have wanted to stop acting out right then and there.

That is why I'm writing this book for you. I want to help you see what consequences lie ahead when you make poor choices early in life. I understand from experience that it's impossible to be able to see this on your own. You may have heard the saying *hindsight is 20/20*. This expression means that after you look back on a situation, you see it differently and realize how you could have done something different.

Writing this book is my way of providing you with hindsight from my life. Maybe you'll see some similarities in your life to what I have gone through. If so, what I share with you throughout this book could change the way you live your life and help you avoid the bad experiences I've had.

I hope you won't have to learn the hard way, as I did. Let's be clear; this is not me telling you what you should do. I'm only sharing experiences of what I know to be true for myself. If you can relate in any way and apply some of the practical strategies I'm sharing, it can make all the difference in shaping your future. My goal is to help you avoid the pitfalls along your journey and give you the knowledge you need to take control of your life.

Remember to stay positive and do your best to avoid the negative side of these at-risk situations. Some of this may not apply to you, and you may be tempted to skip through to other sections of this book. I understand if you do, but I would encourage you to read every page. Even if a particular part doesn't apply to you, it could help you understand what a friend or family member may be going through. You may be able to help someone else by knowing this information. Let's look at some of the most common situations that put you at risk.

BROKEN HOME

You may come from a broken home where only one parent is raising you. If you don't have both a mother and a father figure in your life, this is a sign that you could be at risk for certain bad behaviors due to possible lack of discipline. Both parents bring a unique perspective to a young person's life.

I didn't realize not having a father figure in my life had such an impact on me until it was too late. There are certain things you can learn from one parent that you won't learn from the other. I see this from a new perspective today in the relationship I have with my twelve-year-old stepdaughter and how it differs from the relationship she has with my wife. Sometimes it takes teamwork and requires both parents to solve a specific problem.

My mom did everything she could to accommodate my needs but was ultimately too soft when it came to discipline. She allowed me to do almost anything with no consequences. It didn't occur to me then that not having a father to discipline me would affect my life so much.

DIVORCE OR SEPARATION

If your parents are going through a divorce or separation, there may be a lot of uncertainty in your life. It's between your parents and doesn't affect their love for you. It's their responsibility to work things out to the best of their ability without hurting you. If you misbehave or get into trouble, it will not bring them closer. It may cause them to fight even more.

You may be required to take on more responsibility, like taking care of your siblings. If you are stepping up and doing this, I commend you. You may be living in a negative environment, where there is constant arguing, or maybe your parents are fighting all the time. You may feel as if you just want to get out of the house sometimes, but I would encourage you to stay and try to make the best of the situation. Running isn't the answer, and leaving could make things worse.

Going back and forth between each of your parents in two different houses requires a lot of adjustment. Everything involved in a separation or divorce requires a tremendous amount of adjustment on everyone's part. Unfortunately, the children involved seem to be the ones who suffer the most.

LACK OF EDUCATION

There may be obstacles preventing you from getting a formal education. If you have missed a significant amount of school for any reason, this could be putting you at risk. You may be showing up to school, but if you're not doing the necessary work to get an education, it will have a negative effect on your future.

The good news is that you can self-educate like no other time in history because you have the internet at the tip of your fingers. There are many free resources online for every subject imaginable. I'm going to talk more about these resources throughout this book.

LOSING A PARENT

You may have, unfortunately, lost a parent. He or she may have passed away, or you just simply don't have any relationship with them. When any young person is faced with this situation, it can cause a wide range of issues with lasting effects that can put you at risk.

I want you to know I'm sorry you're in this situation. I can relate, and I will do everything I can to help you understand what you can do to help yourself. In this book, there is an entire chapter on grief and loss to help you learn more about this topic.

BEING RAISED BY SOMEONE OTHER THAN YOUR BIRTH PARENTS

If a grandparent, another family member, a friend's parent, or an adopted family is raising you, it's important to value the relationship with the person or people who are dedicating their lives to help make yours better. Adjusting to these circumstances may not come easy to you, but do your best to show appreciation for what they are doing for you. They are doing their best to fill the shoes of your birth parents.

If you're living in a group home, in foster care, or a foster home with foster parents, this may only be temporary. Do your best to show respect for the system and be on your best behavior to show appreciation for how they're trying to help you find a stable home.

WRAPPING UP THE FIRST CHAPTER

This chapter was to help make you aware of some things which can put you at risk. These topics are by no means a complete list. I'm sure you may have your own specific situations and circumstances that I did not mention. Please accept my apology for not being able to include everything in your personal experience. You are a unique individual, and your situation is unique to you. No one can say they know exactly what you're going through.

These at-risk situations are not roadblocks. They are only speed bumps—signs you will need to mature faster and work harder to help your situation get better. By becoming the best person you can be, you can help yourself overcome these obstacles and live the life of your dreams. I designed this book to help you grow through these challenges and help bring out the true potential you have inside yourself.

Consider getting a notebook to keep handy while you're reading this book. If you're reading a paperback copy of this book, you can write in the margins or any other blank space. Unless this book belongs to a library, please don't write in library books. Write down what you think is putting you at risk and any other ideas that come to mind while reading the pages ahead. Then make a list of what you can personally do to help your situation get better. Writing things down will help you become clear on what you like or don't like about how your life is right now. See if you can find something positive for which to be thankful.

Hopefully, this chapter helped you understand some of the reasons you could be at risk. In the next chapter, I'll discuss the different things you are at risk of having or not having in your life.

CHAPTER 2

THE EFFECTS OF BEING AT RISK

The things that may be putting you at risk can range from minor, easy to fix issues to complicated, more serious issues. You need to understand what you're at risk of because if you're not thinking ahead, you may not care enough to take action now. The things I will talk about in this chapter could determine your future. Taking this seriously or not, could be the difference between spending your life as a career criminal or a successful and happy person.

EDUCATION

You may be at risk of dropping out of school. If that's a choice you make, it could hurt you for the rest of your life. I understand there's a chance you may not like school right now, but that is not a good enough reason to stop going. As I mentioned before, not everything I talk about will apply to you. These are some of the most common situations, and yours may be slightly different. I encourage you to continue reading so you are aware of what could be ahead, even though it may seem far away from where you are now.

For example, if you are only thirteen years old and you love school right now, that's great, and I applaud you. What you may not realize is that when you get older, you could encounter a group of people who seem to be really cool, and they may become your friends. If they skip school, you could be tempted to join them because you want to be part of the cool group.

Skipping individual classes is the way it starts, and before you know it, you're skipping whole days. Then it becomes entire weeks, and the next thing you know, you're expelled from school. You may get discouraged and never want to go back. These actions could cost you an education and future job opportunities.

I've had these experiences. Thankfully, a judge sent me to a court-appointed high school, which was a blessing in disguise. I had two choices—court-appointed school or juvenile detention. Had this not happened to me, I might have dropped out and not gotten a proper education. The coveted high school diploma gave me a ticket to quality jobs and opportunities I wouldn't have had without it since most jobs have minimum requirements for a high school diploma.

If for some reason you didn't receive your high school diploma, you still have an opportunity to get a G.E.D., which is a general education diploma and the equivalent of a high school diploma. However, getting a G.E.D. is much more difficult for most than getting that high school diploma. It's not easy for anyone to go back and take these courses and tests long after they went to school. It takes time, diligence, and hard work, and the job for which they applied may have passed them by before they obtain their G.E.D. Everyone who gets a G.E.D. wishes they had just completed high school when they were younger.

Understand, even though high school may not always be fun, or your favorite pastime, it is a necessity. Don't stop going because of a lack of interest or peer pressure. Being smart is the new cool, and using your brain to get ahead is an attractive quality. Getting an education now will prepare you for future success. Your brain does not stop growing until you are twenty-five years old. Take advantage of this and learn as much as you can now. You can kick back later.

TROUBLE

You may be at risk of getting arrested. When you don't care what happens to you, you may start doing things you shouldn't and ultimately have to pay the price. Getting arrested for minor things is just the beginning, as it was for me. Being expelled from school in the fifth grade should have been a warning for me to be on the lookout for other signs of trouble ahead. Sadly, it wasn't.

When I couldn't afford to buy the things I wanted, I became a thief. I thought it was okay because I was getting something for nothing. It turned out not to be so great once I got caught.

I realize now I could have lived without those things and stayed out of trouble.

The bad habit of stealing starts with small and inexpensive things then graduates to items larger and more expensive. I went through the full spectrum of stealing—from food and clothes to cars and motorcycles. As the cost of the things you steal increases, so do the consequences when you get caught. And thieves always get caught, eventually.

When you get arrested, you will be required to go to court and stand in front of a judge. You will then be ordered to pay for what you stole as well as extra court fees. This payment is called restitution. In addition to restitution, you may be put on probation if you're a first-time offender. With the next arrest, however, you could be sent to juvenile detention.

If you haven't learned your lesson before your eighteenth birthday and continue breaking the law, you will be sent to an adult prison for the same types of charges. These are the things that you can look forward to if you're not careful of your behavior now. Becoming a career criminal is not something anyone should look forward to.

I will talk more about trouble, the consequences of the trouble, and what you can do to avoid getting into a life of crime in a later chapter. For now, I just want you to understand this is something for which you may be at risk.

NO VISION FOR THE FUTURE

You're at risk of not having a plan for your life. You may not realize it, but unless you have a plan, create a vision, and set goals, life will just happen "to" you. In other words, if you fail to start making a plan for your future, you could find yourself waking up on your eighteenth birthday, wondering what you should do and where you should start. I understand that not having a plan isn't a conscious decision, and you may just need a little guidance on how to put a plan together.

I had no plan for my future when I was your age. I never imagined what my eighteenth birthday would look like because I didn't plan to live long enough to see it. I had lost so many friends to violence and other risky behaviors before I was sixteen that I just assumed I would also become a victim of premature death. It's hard to plan for the future when you don't think you have much to live for.

One of the biggest mistakes I ever made was not planning a future for myself. Because of having no plan, I spent my eighteenth birthday in a juvenile detention program. I can't remember who I was with or what I was doing, but I can assure you, there was no party. So, as you can see, life wasn't very important to me. I wasn't prepared to become an adult, continued to break the law, and I found myself in an adult prison only months after being released from the juvenile program.

Please avoid making this mistake. Understand you have so much more to live for. If you take life seriously now, you can wake up on your eighteenth birthday with momentum, ready to go, with a plan in place. You'll be starting your adult life in the best way possible.

I understand it can be hard to look so far ahead, especially if you're only thirteen- or fourteen-years-old right now. Trust me; life goes by fast. Five years is a short amount of time, and it will be gone before you know it. Throughout this book, I will talk about ways you can spend this time effectively, showing you ways to make the most of your teenage years and position yourself for an amazing adult life. There are many things you can do to secure a positive future for yourself.

NO JOB SKILLS

You may be at risk of not having any job skills. The jobs you have as a teenager are only temporary but will provide you with necessary skills and experience. Without developing other skills, you will limit yourself as an adult in the job market. There are many jobs out there, most of which you may not even be aware of.

If you have someone in your life asking you what you want to be when you grow up, this is his or her way of helping you to dream. They wouldn't be asking if they didn't care. Take advantage of this and let someone help you create your plan. It also gives you an opportunity to think about the jobs you may want when you get older.

When you're young, consider every opportunity that comes your way. The jobs you have now will not last forever but will provide you with experience. Learn as you go. You can always develop new skills as you need them.

HAVING A CHILD

You may also be at risk of having a child while you're still a teenager. If you're not careful, this could happen to you, and your life will never be the same. Imagine how your life would be different if you had to raise a child of your own.

Think about how hard it is to take care of yourself. Now think about taking care of another human being. Not all teenage parents have problems, but most of them don't stay together for the long term. Unless you have a plan and know you really care for the other parent of your child, it's often not going to last.

If you have a child and don't stay with your partner, your child then becomes at risk because a single teenage parent will be raising him or her. You have the power to break the cycle and avoid future generations from having to experience the same circumstances you may be in now.

Boys and girls both share this same responsibility. Be safe and protect yourself. Don't let one night of fun impact the rest of your life.

HAVING NO RESPECT

You are at risk of growing up with no respect for authority. These authority figures include adults, members of law enforcement, teachers, bosses, and anyone else in your life who you feel is looking down on you. If this type of behavior has been an issue for you, there are things you can do to change it, control it, and accept the unique roles people have in your life. Teachers are here to provide you with an education; parents are here to help raise you right by setting rules and boundaries, and bosses are here to do their jobs and make sure you do yours.

Try not to think people are always out to get you or are intentionally trying to do you wrong. It's important for you to show respect for all authority in the many ways it presents itself in your life. The sooner you realize this, and the sooner you accept this, the easier your life will be.

BEING ANGRY

You're at risk of being angry all the time. You may not realize why you are angry or who you are angry with. These feelings could cause you to take it out on the wrong people. Some reasons you may be angry are: You may feel as if you've been dealt a bad hand in life. You may feel as if everyone else has it better than you. You may feel as if everyone is out to get you.

I assure you these are not all true. Even if some of these things are true, it doesn't justify you hurting other people, whether it be physically or mentally. You have a right to be angry. Yes, I understand this, but there are ways to harness and redirect your anger into more positive things.

If you're so angry that you're always looking for a fight, you'll always find one. Fighting leads to trouble, and trouble leads to a miserable life. In the next chapter, I will dive deeper into the topic of anger.

CHAPTER 3

How Anger Affects You

I was angry for most of my childhood and well into my adult life. This anger was destroying me. Going through life angry and having a chip on your shoulder are stressful ways to live. Because I have lived it, I understand the problems anger can cause at a young age. Any of the circumstances I discussed in the last chapter could cause someone to become angry and, it's understandable.

What you're going through may not seem fair, but the fact of the matter is you're still here. You can control your future if you take action now. Reading this book and others like it is an excellent place to start.

When you become angry, frustrated, impatient, and lose your temper, it affects your ability to make accurate decisions. Becoming angry begins the domino effect of the negative results you are getting in your life. Learning how to control your anger will dramatically improve the quality of your life.

DISRESPECT

Disrespecting people could be your way of projecting your anger towards someone else—someone who likely isn't even the reason you're angry. These actions cause tension and bad feelings between you and the person you disrespect. Why would you take your anger out on an innocent person?

I know this is what I did. I walked around with a chip on my shoulder for the first half of my life, because I thought the world owed me something. I felt like I was cheated out of a fair chance at life, and I was angry about it. I disrespected people because I didn't care.

When you're angry, it's easy to lash out at the people around you, but these are often the people who love you and want to help you the most. Sometimes you just have to let go of the anger and let your guard down. Purposely being disrespectful to people and causing them to turn away from you is not the answer. This behavior may be a natural defense mechanism, but lashing out in anger always does more harm than good.

GUILT

Stop holding on to any guilt you may have. Guilt will cause you to become angry. If you blame yourself, you'll find your conscience becomes so heavy it keeps you from doing everything else in your life. It's best not to walk around with a guilty conscience.

Guilt will cause you stress and affect other areas of your life, including your physical and mental health. This can include anxiety, depression, loss of appetite, and lack of sleep, just to name a few. The stress from guilt could lead to negative behaviors, such as smoking or using drugs and alcohol, because you may think they will relieve your painful feelings, but they won't. This is why it is so crucial for you to address these issues now before things get out of control.

I will cover more on these topics throughout this book to help you better understand how they're all connected.

BLAME

Your anger may cause you to blame other people for everything you perceive is wrong in your life. When you stop blaming others for whatever situation you are in and start taking responsibility for your own actions and what you can control, you'll find you're not nearly as angry. If it's something over which you have no control, then the only way to not be angry is to let it go and not stress about it.

It's a different story if someone legitimately deserves the blame for something. I'm not suggesting you accept blame for something you didn't do. What I am saying is that if you're put in a bad situation because of someone else, accept the responsibility of finding a way to make things better for yourself. Continuing to blame them won't improve the situation. It will only cause you more anger.

REDIRECTING THE ANGER

Find ways and outlets to let your anger go in a positive way. My hope is you will see how anger is affecting your life. Once you realize this, you can control it. Controlling your anger may not come easy for you in the beginning. Pay attention to how anger affects your behavior. You can harness this energy and use it to motivate you.

For example, if you're angry at the way the environment is being treated, you can redirect this anger into becoming an activist for climate change. If you're mad because your school doesn't provide the lunch you want, you could attend the next school board meeting and give a presentation on how to make the lunches better.

Finding creative ways to use this energy will be a conscious decision you need to make. This change will not come without effort. You are not alone in having anger. Everyone is angry about something; you just may not see it. Some people are better at controlling it than others.

ANGER CAUSES TROUBLE

Your anger can get you in trouble in various ways, some of which you may not understand right now. This anger may be the root cause of many of your problems. When you're mad at the world, you're always looking for trouble. You want to fight everyone you see at the drop of a hat. Yes, I am talking about physical violence. If this is not an issue for you, congratulations. This may give you an insight into why some of your friends are always fighting.

Fighting people on the street can get you arrested. If you have an issue with fighting, here are some alternative ways you can deal with your aggression: You can become a boxer or mixed martial arts fighter. You can take karate lessons or any of the martial arts disciplines.

Some form of anger is almost always the cause of fighting. There are physical and verbal ways people express their anger. Constantly arguing with people can cause you to get in trouble too. This can be a problem with your friends or adults in your life. Think about the ways you get in trouble in school or at home when you're angry. You can control this by listening to what people have to say and having a relaxed attitude in your response. Try not to always be on the defensive.

IDENTIFYING THE TRIGGERS

Consider keeping a journal and writing about what makes you angry and why. Your journal is for your eyes only; no one else needs to see it. This exercise of writing it down will help you track what causes your anger issues. It will be helpful for you to go back through your journal and see the different times you got angry. You'll know where you were, who you were with, and what you were doing. You may then start to see a pattern.

There may be certain people you spend time with who make you mad. There may be certain places you frequently visit that cause your anger to come out. It will be helpful to identify the source of your frustration. Knowing what makes you angry is half the battle.

Once you know your triggers, you can create a plan to avoid them. You can replace those negative things with positive ones. No person or place is worth losing your happiness. I will talk about hobbies and ideas for things you can do and ways to spend your time later in this book.

TREATMENT

If working on your anger issues by yourself isn't helping you, I recommend you consider professional anger management treatment. You can go to group therapy, or you can see an individual counselor who can help you get your anger issues under control. Ask the adult in your life to help you get connected with an anger management counselor or group. Don't let your anger control you. The sooner you gain control of it, the better your life will be.

CHAPTER 4

UNDERSTANDING GRIEF AND LOSS

G rief is a natural process of experiencing internal pain when you lose someone or something you love. Mourning, on the other hand, is the way you express this pain on the outside.

Loss can come in several forms. People tend to first think of grief and loss when associated with death. Losing friends or family may be one of the more familiar senses of loss, but it's not the only thing that causes grief in someone's life. In this chapter, I will touch on occupational, social, and physical losses. The way loss comes is different for everyone, and all losses take various amounts of time to heal. Not all people experience loss from death early in their lives.

OCCUPATIONAL LOSS

Occupational loss can occur if someone loses his or her job. This loss could happen to one of your parents. It can be devastating when a person has worked at the same company or has done a specific type of work for an extended period of time. It's important to be empathetic to your parent's situation. You may not understand if you have never had this personal experience, but losing a job can happen to anybody at any time.

This time in history has been especially difficult, as I am writing this book while under a stay-at-home order during the 2020 global pandemic. Over forty million Americans have lost their jobs in the past few months, creating the most significant job loss in the country's history. Your parent may have been a victim of this crisis. If so, try to help keep that parent in good spirits and provide support.

If this happens to you, surround yourself with positive people—those who will be supportive and helpful in letting you know everything will eventually be okay.

It's normal for someone who goes through a significant, life-changing event to feel stress and a sense of loss. Unfortunately, sometimes this stress is taken out on people who don't deserve it. It's important that you try not to make others suffer because of how you feel. If someone is taking their frustrations out on you, explain to them how it makes you feel. If they apologize, accept the apology and move on. Don't hold a grudge. Grudges don't hurt the other person; they only make you more miserable. Be compassionate instead. It may be their way of grieving.

When this type of loss occurs, you feel a range of emotions and uncertainty. Even the smallest loss can feel significant at the moment. Take comfort in knowing when one door closes, another one opens, and things will get better. Being optimistic and staying positive can help make things better.

SOCIAL LOSS

Social grief can occur when you lose connections to friends. It's not the same as if someone passes away, but it's a loss all the same. You'll learn that friends come and go throughout life. If someone is your best friend or your boyfriend or girlfriend, there will be a much stronger connection to them than someone who is just an acquaintance.

When you have an argument that is serious enough to cause the loss of a close friend, you will experience grief. You should express that grief outwardly and not bottle it up. Find someone with whom you can share your feelings. Talk about it, and don't be afraid or ashamed to accept the love and support from others.

People change, and you may not like the person they become. It may become necessary for you to decide whether or not to stay friends with someone you don't like anymore. Everyone changes; it's part of the life cycle. New people will come in and out of your life throughout your lifetime. You have to be flexible and willing to adapt to different people and different situations as they change in your life.

You will also change, causing people not to recognize you. As you become a better person, people who are looking for the old you may not want to hang out with you anymore. Once you no longer have anything in common with a person, the relationship may fade away. If you're aware of the possibility these things will happen, you'll be better prepared to handle them when they do.

If a friend moves away, you can continue the relationship in a new way. With cell phones, the different social networking platforms, and other technologies available today, keeping in touch is easy. There's no reason to lose touch with someone you care about because of the physical distance between you.

As a young person, it's often out of your control when your family decides to relocate or move to a new house. I know it can be stressful for you, and you may not fully understand why it has to happen. I'm sure if this has happened to you, the adults in your life have had a good reason for it. Adults are thinking of your best interest when considering a big move. Usually, this happens for a better job opportunity or to get closer to other family members.

I know it can be an adjustment, but change can be good. You never know who you're going to meet at any time in life. The next person could become your new best friend.

PHYSICAL LOSS

There is no time limit on how long it will take to grieve the loss of a human life. No one can tell you how long this pain will last. In some cases, it will last a lifetime. How you respond will determine the difference between going into a depression or deciding to live your life with a new purpose.

The closer a person is to you, the harder it will be when you lose them. Think about how this person would want you to live and try to go forward in a way that you think would make them happy. Moving on with your life doesn't mean forgetting about the life of your lost loved one.

You can choose to honor their memory by living your life with a purpose they would admire. You could fulfill whatever dreams they might have had, if possible. You could start a foundation in their memory to create awareness to whatever caused their death. You could become passionate about finding a cure to prevent others from having the same experience. These are just a few ideas to get you thinking in a positive direction.

I have dealt with an enormous amount of loss in my life. I had the unfortunate experience of losing both of my parents. I have also lost many other family members and a significant number of friends, coworkers, and acquaintances. I have personally attended over fifty funerals and have known well over one hundred people who have passed away.

As you get older, more people you know will pass away. This is an unfortunate reality. Make the most of the time you have with your family and friends. Create memories you will be able to cherish for the rest of your life. Always remember the good times. Take a lot of pictures, smile, and be happy. Save souvenirs and keepsakes of the memories you create with the people you love. Remember the laughter you share and create memorable impressions in your heart and mind that nobody can ever take away from you.

STAGES OF GRIEF

There are seven stages of grief. I will list them here with a brief description. I would encourage you to do more research and learn more about these topics if they apply to you. There are many books written on this subject.

Stage one - Shock or Disbelief. Your initial reaction when you first receive the news, and you are literally in shock. You can't believe the news is true, so you have a hard time believing it.

Stage two – Denial. Where you just want things to be how they were. You don't want to believe this is reality, and you are hoping it's just a bad dream.

Stage three – Bargaining. Asking yourself what you could have done differently. What if certain things were different? What if this person did something different?

Stage four – Guilt. When you might start to believe it's your fault.

Stage five – Anger. Your underlying pain causes it. Anger is a common emotion when losing someone or something.

Stage six – Depression. A period of sadness, irritability, low motivation, feeling worthless, and feeling hopeless.

Stage seven - Acceptance or Hope. You're learning to live with the loss you have experienced. Accepting there is nothing you can do to change what has happened. Knowing you have much to live for through hope and faith.

HELPING YOURSELF HEAL

There are many ways you can take the emotions you're feeling and turn them into a positive in your life. Whether you are grieving the loss of a person, a job, a social group, or moving away from your friends, there is no one magic piece of advice to make it all better. Each situation will require a different remedy.

Do your best to turn your attention to something positive that will help to create joy in your life. There are various things you can do with your time to take your mind off of any situation. I will address a list of things that might be helpful in the hobbies chapter of this book.

One of the most beneficial ways you can help to make yourself feel better is by learning to laugh again. Laughter is a tool you can use to lift your emotions and create happiness. Simply smiling more can help boost your mood and change the way you carry yourself. Doing this can give you a more energetic personality and bring you back to your true self.

When you are genuinely enjoying something, it is hard to think negatively. You can find laughter in many ways—watching funny videos, reading humorous books, or watching a stand-up comedian. Any form of comedy will help.

I want you to know you are not alone. If you are having a tough time with a specific type of grief or loss, I encourage you to seek professional help. You could look into a support group related to your personal experience or an individual counselor, therapist, or group therapy.

There are many phone and online resources available to you. Not all consultations require you to be face to face with somebody.

Whatever your situation, keep your head up, do your best to think positively, envision a great future for yourself, and live your life with purpose.

Disclaimer: This is not medical advice; I am not a licensed counselor or doctor. This information is based on my personal experiences and techniques I have used to help myself over the years.

CHAPTER 5

ADAPTING TO YOUR LIVING SITUATION

A family does not always mean blood relatives. The people who love you, care for you, and want the best for you are most important. Do everything you can to be a positive contributor and make the best of any situation in the place you are living in. No family unit is perfect; each one is unique in its own way.

LIVING IN CHAOS

You may live in a house with two parents who are always fighting. Try not to choose sides or get involved. Show you care and say how much you love them both. Encourage them to make peace for the sake of your family. Make suggestions for things you can do together as a family that might bring them closer together. Go through pictures with them to remind them of how happy they were in the past.

It may be that your parents work all the time, leaving you home to take care of everything. You may see yourself as the man or woman of the house right now. These responsibilities could include taking care of yourself and your siblings, helping them with eating, bathing, and getting ready for school. If you are, I commend you for stepping up and doing what you know is right. This role can be beneficial training for when you get older and also provide insight into what it's like to be a parent.

SHARED CUSTODY

When parents are divorced or separated, you may have to live between two houses. This change can take some time to get used to. You now must pack up whenever it is time to visit the other parent. Often you may not want to go. Sometimes this must happen because of a court order, not by choice of the parents. If you understand this, it may be easier for you to accept the change.

At your new second home, making friends can be uncomfortable at first, but don't let it stop you. If you focus on the positive, this change can be good. New scenery and a change of pace can be a breath of fresh air. Often, parents will do extra things to make you happy during this transition period. Take advantage of this one-on-one time and suggest doing some fun things together. If you can't change the situation, try to make the best of it.

BLENDED FAMILY

You may be a part of a blended family. There could come a time when your mother or father has a new boyfriend or girlfriend, husband, or wife, who also has children that will become a part of your family. Living with a new adult, and possibly kids may be uncomfortable for you at first. You may not automatically like this person or people. If this person makes your parent happy, try to support him or her and find the positives in the situation.

There are many reasons your parent may invite a new person into your home. It's important for you to understand your parent has your best interest in mind when doing this. Adults have bills to pay, and sometimes when two adults are dating for a while and getting serious, it makes financial sense to live together. Living separately, they have two sets of bills. When one person is spending more time at the other's house, it just makes sense for them to share one set of bills instead of two.

When an adult has a car payment, rent, or mortgage on a house, utility bills, insurances, food, and clothing bills, it can become expensive. It's especially difficult for a single person with one job to meet all the financial needs of raising kids. Having a second income in the household can provide financial security. Combining two homes into one can be the difference in deciding where you can afford to live and what school you will attend.

I know this can be a real challenge, but look at the big picture to see how this could help your overall situation. Respect the role of this new person. Purposely driving him or her away can make things more difficult and cause more division in your new family. Make every attempt to get to know your parent's new partner and give things a chance to work.

LIVING WITH SOMEONE OTHER THAN YOUR BIRTH PARENTS

Whether it's your grandparent, aunt, uncle, friend's parent, or someone else who is assuming the role of your guardian, respect the adult in your life who is taking care of you. By putting a roof over your head, this shows they care. They want to see you become a better person. Let them assist you with your schoolwork and help you get an education. Think about what they are sacrificing to do this for you. Always be thankful for all the people who are doing their best to support you. Accept any resources and help they are willing to provide.

Embrace what you have. Show appreciation to the people who are taking care of you. Be respectful and follow their rules. Trying hard in school, staying out of trouble, avoiding the use of profanity, and being helpful around the house are all things you can control. These are the basic ways to show you care about them and yourself.

BEING RAISED BY A SYSTEM

If you are currently incarcerated in a juvenile facility, have been placed in a foster home, or similar type of program, appreciate the system taking care of you. Have respect for the people who are working hard to take care of you, regardless of who they are and what your relationship is to them. If you have a roof over your head, be thankful. Many kids are homeless and hungry, living on the street.

It's important to be grateful, even when you don't think what you have is much. If you're in a system right now, the one thing you can control is your attitude about the situation. If you're optimistic and think positive, you'll attract positive things to you. Focus on what you can control.

Do your best to avoid making the situation worse. I saw this happen when I was in a juvenile program. People give up hope and get themselves into more trouble. It is also common for someone else to sabotage your success, so don't let other people drag you down. Getting into a fight can result in you being given more time in the place you don't want to be. Disrespecting staff members can only make your time there more miserable. Avoid letting other people's negativity affect your behavior.

Dream about what you want your future to look like, then create a plan for how you can make it happen. Focus on becoming a better person in every way possible. Try to understand your situation is temporary and better days are ahead.

LIVING ON YOUR OWN

For whatever reason, you may be taking care of yourself but temporarily living with a friend. Now your goal is to get your own place to live. Before you venture out on your own, there are some things you'll need to know. There is more on this topic in other sections of this book, including the chapter on taking care of yourself and the money chapter. Let's start with creating your plan to be out on your own.

You'll need to start by getting a job so that you'll have money, and you should save as much as possible. Let's assume you'll live alone. A small apartment will be a good start. For a decent place, most require first and last months' rent, plus a security deposit, usually equal to a month's rent before you can move in. This amount is a total of three months' rent you will need to secure your new apartment.

You may need to sign a lease for a specific amount of time, six months, or a year. If you're still under the age of eighteen, you may need an adult to cosign for you. Ask someone you trust who will be willing to help you in this way. You'll also need to put the utility bills in your name. These expenses could include electricity, water, gas, and the internet. Some of those require an up-front deposit also.

Another option would be for you to find an apartment where the owner would give you a month-to-month lease. In this instance, you may get lucky and find one that includes all the utilities, which would mean one monthly payment that covers everything. It may also mean you don't have to put up the security deposit or last month's rent. You may be able to move in with only one month's rent upfront.

You could also rent a room in a house with other people. You would share a bathroom and kitchen with strangers. These types of places are usually cheap, and you get what you pay for. I would consider this one as a last resort, but if you have nothing else, it will get you off the street. If you must start with this option, start saving immediately and be looking to upgrade as soon as possible to your own apartment.

Your budget and which option you choose will determine where you would want to look for this new living space. You can start by looking in the newspaper, which usually lists rooms and apartments for rent in the classified section. You can also search online for places in your desired area.

When you find something you like, call and ask questions about what type of costs will be associated with moving in. And be sure to ask which utilities will be included. You'll also want to know if there will be a credit check or criminal background check. If you have a criminal record, be honest with the owner/lessee, and they may be more understanding and appreciate your honesty. However, if you lie, and they check your record, nothing you say will win their trust back.

A credit check involves looking at your history of paying bills on time. You will learn more about credit in the Money chapter of this book. Not all places do these types of checks. That's why it's important to ask up front, so you don't get too excited about a new home and then learn that it's not a realistic option for you.

If you have the option to live with family, stay, and make the best of it. Living on your own can be great, but it can also become expensive and lonely. Whatever situation you're in, I hope this information is helpful. Make the best of what you have and appreciate the people willing to help you along the way.

CHAPTER 6

FRIENDSHIP QUALITIES

P eople who disrespect you do not deserve your friendship. These people may be your acquaintances, but they are not your real friends. You need to realize your worth. Surround yourself with people who share the same values as you.

TRUST AND RESPECT

Trust and respect are important in creating a strong foundation in a friendship or relationship. If you know these things up front, it will help you make better decisions when choosing friends.

Be careful not to be influenced by peer pressure. If people value and respect you, they will not put this kind of pressure on you. If you go against your instincts, it will often lead to a regrettable decision.

Having these things in place will allow you to be comfortable talking to someone on a personal level. You won't have to worry about what they'll say or do with the information you share with them when you're not around. If you share personal information with someone who doesn't respect you, they might pass that information along to others.

You should also carry the same values toward their personal information. When someone shares something personal with you, it's essential to keep this information to yourself. Once you break someone's trust, that person will never see you the same way again. Think about how you feel when someone does this to you.

DON'T CHANGE TO FIT IN

Be yourself. Don't change who you are just to fit in. Yes, change is essential and can benefit you, if you're doing it for the right reasons. Changing only to please someone else wouldn't be the real you. This will cause you misery and awkwardness when trying to put on a persona just to impress other people.

Accept yourself for who you are and accept other people for who they are. We are all different in our own ways. Having common interests brings people together. Don't judge people because of how they look. Get to know someone before deciding what you think of them.

Be confident in yourself. When you're fake, people can see through it. Would you like it if someone only pretended to be interested in you and your hobbies? Imagine how betrayed you would feel if you found out after months, or even years, that he or she was not the person you thought they were.

FINDING LIKE-MINDED PEOPLE

When you spend time with people who think like you, it creates the most natural relationship. You will find that this will be where you are most happy. People who share the same positive interests, goals, hobbies, and values can become better friends. The more you have in common with people, the easier it is to get along with them.

Like-minded people can be those who share the same vision as you. They have a similar outlook on life and share your images of the future. Aligning yourself with those who share the same interests creates a better chance of a lasting relationship.

AVOIDING NEGATIVITY

It isn't always easy to avoid negative people but do your best to limit the amount of time you spend listening to their negativity. Some people have nothing nice to say and are always looking at the downside. They are known as pessimists. Look for positive qualities in people you desire to have as friends.

People are not the only form of negativity to watch out for. Be careful about how much time you spend watching the local news, social media videos, or any other source of negativity. This information can cause fear and doubt. Negativity can only affect you if you let it get into your head. You can limit negative information by focusing your attention on positive things.

If someone is giving you positive comments and encouragement, these are clues you should spend more time with this person. Have self-confidence and accept his or her compliments. That person might see the positive in you before you can see it in yourself. Surround yourself with supportive people. Negative people will drain your energy.

FAKE SOCIAL MEDIA FRIENDS

Social media is full of fake people hiding behind their keyboards, acting like someone they're not. Be aware of people online who want to make friends with you. If you have never met a person face to face, be skeptical until you have proof that they are telling you the truth about who they are.

In some situations, it may be okay to make friends online, but never give them any personal or private information about yourself. Be careful and do your best to check who these people are before becoming too friendly with them.

When possible, I encourage you to get out of the house and into the real world and meet people face to face. This can be through a variety of ways, depending on what your hobbies and interest are. Maybe you will do this in school through sports or music.

Music lessons, the local library, skate parks, and dance studios are all great places to make friends. Obviously, you will know they have the same interests as you if they are there too. If you get out into public settings and socialize through your shared interest groups, you'll make friends. These are people you can get to know personally.

It's nice to have friends you can spend time with in person. I understand that you may feel socially awkward, but I encourage you to get out of your comfort zone and take a chance. Be cautious not to let your guard down too quickly, but get out, socialize, and go for it.

CREATING YOUR OWN CIRCLES

If you have an interest in something but can't find a group that exists for it, consider creating your own group. It can be for whatever your interests are. Maybe you want to start a book club and meet at the local library. If you like to ride skateboards, start a group that meets at the skate park every Wednesday at a specific time. If you want to do ceramics or create arts and crafts and there is no other local group around, consider becoming the leader and starting one.

These things I just talked about will inspire teamwork. If you start your group with one person, it can grow to several. Then you'll have many minds working together toward the same goal. This teamwork will ignite your imagination. You can consider this a mastermind group.

Many successful businesses have been built on the foundation of mastermind groups. When multiple people get together, focused on the same goal, there are better results. You can gain much power and knowledge from the wisdom of other people.

Make a list of groups you would like to be part of, then do some research to see if any already exist in your local area. When you have completed your research, you can look at your list and decide if you want to join an existing group or start your own. Creating and organizing a new group can be a positive way to spend your time. You will learn, grow, and take your mind off any negative things going on in your life.

CHANGING YOUR WAYS

Your interests will change as you grow older. When you live a different lifestyle, your friends may change too. Your best friends will still be there, but you'll always be making new friends as you experience new things. These experiences will often be through jobs, hobbies, or mutual friends.

As you develop into the best version of yourself, you'll start to dream about doing things that seem impossible. When you tell other people about these dreams, they may doubt you can achieve them. Don't be discouraged by this. Stay focused and understand that not everyone will believe in your vision. It doesn't mean what they say is true; it just means you need to find more positive people with whom to share your vision. Don't change your vision or goals just because someone says you can't do it.

You'll find people who will be supportive. You can do anything you put your mind to, and it's always much easier when you have someone who supports you. You increase your odds of achieving success when you share your vision with like-minded people.

When people laugh at your goals or dreams, don't let it negatively affect you. They're just jealous because of not having any hopes of their own or simply want to be mean. These are not the type of people you want to be around. Remember, there is a difference between a friend and an acquaintance.

CHAPTER 7

YOUR PHYSICAL WELL-BEING

Your overall physical health is especially important. You may not think much about it because you feel healthy now. That may not always be the case as you get older. You can experience many types of health issues, most of which can be avoided if you're aware of what to do to prevent them and if you take good care of yourself today.

There could be some genetic health concerns in your family. You should ask older adults about your family's health history. By knowing that, you will be able to watch for any signs of hereditary diseases and take preventive measures. Some examples are heart disease, cancers, or diabetes, to name a few. For example, if you have a family history of heart disease, you can watch your cholesterol and exercise more to help reduce your risk.

Smoking of any kind will increase your chances of illness. It will also cause your teeth to turn yellow. Avoid starting this bad habit or quit now if you've already started. Not smoking is one of the most important health decisions you can make for yourself.

BEING HEALTH CONSCIOUS

One reason I never paid much attention to my health was that I wasn't expecting to live very long. As a teenager, I didn't have a vision for my future. My friends were dying young, and I just assumed I would be a victim of premature death too.

Before I was out of my teens, I'd been shot at five different times and figured I was more likely to die from gun violence than a heart attack. So, I ate whatever greasy foods I wanted, along with doing many other unhealthy things. Here I am at forty-two years old, wishing I had done things differently regarding the way I took care of my health. I never exercised and spent my teenage years hanging on street corners, eating pizza and cheesesteaks, smoking, and drinking beer. Please take care of yourself better than I did.

You may be having a hard time seeing yourself living a long, prosperous life. If this is your mindset, I encourage you to change it. Create a long-term vision for your life. You can live longer by taking care of yourself at an early age. The good habits you create now can stay with you forever if you choose. If you develop a habit of eating healthy, exercising regularly, and taking care of your physical body, you're increasing your chances of living much longer.

Your future is much brighter than you may imagine. Your current circumstances don't need to define how the rest of your life will be. Focusing on your health and taking better care of yourself now will help you live a better life. It will also increase your energy, creativity, and overall well-being.

HAVING A HEALTHY BODY

You only get one body, so take excellent care of it. Harming your body by physically abusing it will come back to affect you later in life. For example, if you break bones now, the bones could ache for the rest of your life. Try to be careful of what you do and take precautions to avoid physically hurting your body in any way.

Being careful to avoid harm also includes being mindful of the way risky behaviors will affect your body. For example, if you want to ride a skateboard, be aware of potential risks. Be careful and always wear a helmet, knee pads, and other protective gear. You might watch a few videos or take some lessons on how to ride better before getting started.

When you become an adult, you'll be responsible for your own medical insurance. Health insurance is often expensive and rarely covers one hundred percent of all costs. One way you can avoid having expensive health care bills is by taking better care of your body now. Some examples of these are basic things you probably already realize, but may not be doing.

EYE CARE

If your eyesight is poor, or your eyes are always bothering you, you should see an eye doctor. If an eye doctor recommends that you wear glasses, I suggest you do so. Yes, I understand you may be self-conscious about wearing glasses. Don't let the thought of people making fun of you be discouraging. If you have prescription glasses, you should wear them. If you're not wearing them when you're supposed to, your eyesight will get worse. Your vision is critical, and you shouldn't let your looks affect whether or not you wear glasses.

Aside from a short-term issue I had from being sprayed with mace by the police, I've been fortunate to have twenty-twenty vision most of my life. A couple of years ago, around my fortieth birthday, I received the gift of eye problems. My doctor tells me it comes with the territory. The best thing for me to do is continue to get checked yearly and change prescriptions as needed. Now I wear glasses all day, every day because it helps me see better, and makes my eyes feel better.

I'm not concerned with the way I look in my glasses. I chose frames I like, and you will be able to also. You could consider wearing contact lenses if you're self-conscious about the way you may look in glasses. Just make the decision, one way or another, to correct your vision when or if it becomes necessary.

DENTAL HYGIENE

Taking care of your teeth is something you can control. We have all been taught to brush and floss our teeth since we were little kids. Unfortunately, many of us have ignored this advice. I was guilty of this as a young person. That did not seem important to me. I didn't realize how much this neglect would cost me as an adult. Looking back, I wish I had paid more attention to my dental hygiene and done more brushing and flossing.

In my early twenties, besides having cavities, I also needed to get root canals done on two different teeth. Even though I had good health insurance, it only covered fifty percent of the cost. Most insurances don't cover the full cost of specialized dental work. After my insurance covered the first fifty percent, I was responsible for paying the remaining balance, which was over four hundred dollars for each tooth. The money was a small price to pay to make the pain go away, but I could've avoided it by having better dental hygiene as a kid.

You may think, *Well, I just don't feel like brushing or flossing.* I felt the same way. Brushing and flossing your teeth should become a habit you start now and continue forever. Three times a day is great, but two times should be a minimum, in the morning and at night. It's also a good idea to have a dentist clean your teeth every six months.

Many new technologies are making this process a lot easier, for example, electric toothbrushes and water flossers. You also don't need to use the old-fashioned style dental floss. There are these little U-shaped flossers on the end of toothbrushes, making it so much easier to get into the back of your mouth. Regularly using mouthwash can also be an enormous help. You may think this can be annoying and time-consuming, but it's well worth it and will save you a lot of pain, aggravation, and money down the road.

HEALTHY EATING AND EXERCISE

Your habits of exercising and eating healthy should go hand in hand. They work best when done together. If you eat fast food, greasy foods, and junk food all the time, it will negatively affect your physical health in several ways. Exercising regularly and taking care of your physical body are essential. When you exercise for an hour and then go straight to eating fatty foods, it's counterproductive.

Managing weight is a struggle for much of our population. Some people are always trying to lose weight, and some wish they could gain weight. Your goals will depend on your situation. Either way, healthy foods are better for your overall well-being.

There are many choices for healthy food. I'm sure you can find a variety of foods you'll enjoy. Don't be afraid to try new things. Do more research about what will work best for you. Regardless of whether you are big or small or consider yourself underweight or overweight, eating healthy and exercising is good for everyone.

The exercise routine you create for yourself will depend on your health goals. Exercise routines are unique to every person. You can get ideas from other people and create your own system. Your routine can be as simple as walking for a certain amount of time each day or doing a cardio exercise in your bedroom. Don't think you must go to a professional gym to get healthy. Creating a healthy lifestyle will benefit you long term and will help you feel better about yourself too.

SLEEP

Sleep is underrated when thinking about your health. Your body restores and rejuvenates while you're sleeping. Sleeping helps improve your memory, reduces your stress levels, and can help fight against some diseases. Your body needs a certain amount of rest every day. A teenager needs an average of eight to ten hours of sleep per night. The amount of sleep your body requires can differ based on your exact age.

The quality of your sleep will affect all areas of your health, including both your mental and physical health. Getting the proper amount of sleep can be one of the best things you can do to maintain overall good health. You can learn a lot about the way you feel by learning more about the benefits of sleep.

DRINKING WATER

Drinking water is one of the easiest ways to keep your body healthy. Most people don't drink enough water. How much you should drink depends on your gender, age, and weight. There are charts you can use to find out how much you should drink every day.

When you don't drink enough water, your body becomes dehydrated. This can cause you to become dizzy, lightheaded, confused, and not feel well. It can also have a negative effect on your energy levels. Other benefits of drinking water are that it helps hydrate your skin, it regulates your body temperature, it flushes toxins from your body and much more. Get into the habit of drinking more water, and you will physically feel better throughout your day.

Combining all the topics in this chapter will help you feel better and improve the quality of your life now and well into the future. When you feel good, you'll be a happier person.

CHAPTER 8

THE DANGERS OF DRUGS AND ALCOHOL

Using any form of drugs or alcohol will only make matters worse for any situation you are in. They are bad for your health and will cause more problems than they are worth. Avoiding these things will give you a much greater chance of living a happy and successful life. If you've never tried these things, don't start now. If you have just experimented, make a decision to stop today. You don't need any more odds stacked against you.

USING WILL NOT MAKE YOUR PROBLEMS DISAPPEAR

I understand you may have issues or problems. You may think by using an illegal substance, all of your troubles will go away. I assure you this is not the case, and it will make your problems worse. You will wake up the next day, realizing your problems are still there, you feel like crap, and you don't have any money in your pocket.

Often you won't be able to remember what you did the night before. There is no worse feeling than waking up in a jail cell and not remembering what you did that got you there. Now you have a whole new set of problems to deal with, in addition to the things you were trying to forget. You might wake up injured in a hospital bed, not knowing why. If you do remember, it doesn't make things any better. You'll feel ashamed. Trust me; I've learned these lessons the hard way.

PEER PRESSURE

Don't fall for peer pressure. Do what you know is right, and walk away. You may think something is cool to do because other people are doing it. This isn't the case. The people you think are cool will end up getting themselves in trouble. You don't want to go along with them for this ride. Doing something because you think it's popular and it will win you some points with the cool group doesn't mean it will be a smart thing for you to do.

Before today, you may have had an excuse to say you didn't know these things were bad for you. Now you know, and the decisions are yours to make. You're on your own when something bad happens to you. Your cool friends will be nowhere to be found.

They will run and leave you to take the blame. It always comes down to every person for himself when doing illegal things.

SMOKING AND VAPING

I know it's popular among teenagers to vape or smoke cigarettes. Smoking of any kind is an expensive and dirty habit. This includes vaping. There are many misconceptions about whether it's healthier to smoke or vape. Let's be clear; neither one is healthy nor good for you. Even if you could figure out which one was better, you would only be choosing the lesser of two evils. Both will harm your body and cost you money—money that you could put to much better use.

Most products associated with smoking and vaping contain nicotine, which is addictive. You don't want to become addicted to anything bad for you. Just because something is legal doesn't make it a good decision to do it. Become addicted to reading books instead.

You want to live as long as possible, and these things will be working against you. Smoking of any kind causes major health problems—problems such as heart disease, lung cancer, and many other things that can kill you over time. Heart disease is one of the leading causes of death in America. Although there are many forms of cancer, lung cancer is at the top of the list for deaths caused by cancer.

ALCOHOL

Drinking alcohol of any kind is bad for you and illegal until you're twenty-one years old in America. It is so highly addictive; even then, I wouldn't recommend you doing it. You may think it's cool if your friends are trying it. Again, this doesn't make it right.

If you drink a lot of alcohol, you can develop alcoholism, and your body will begin to depend on it, just as with any other drug addiction. Keep in mind that alcoholism is the leading cause of liver disease that can eventually lead to death.

When I was young, teenage drinking parties caused me a lot of problems and aggravation. Every time I got arrested for underage drinking, along with spending a night in jail, I had to pay fines, attend underage drinking classes, do community service, and had a suspension put on the driver's license I didn't even have yet. If you're lucky enough to have a driver's license, your driving privileges will be suspended. If you are not old enough to get your driver's license, underage drinking arrests will lead to a suspension placed on your future license. This action means if you can get your license at age sixteen, an underage drinking arrest will delay your eligibility.

I had racked up so many underage drinking charges, that I didn't get my driver's license until I was twenty years old. This was four years after the law legally allowed me to get a license in the state of Pennsylvania. I could have gotten my driver's license at sixteen years old like everyone else, had I not chosen to be drinking when I was underage. Losing the ability to have a driver's license kept me stuck in the city. I took trains and buses, but there's nothing like the freedom of getting in a car and being able to drive yourself wherever you want to go.

Once you become eighteen, a driver's license and legal vehicle are your tickets to freedom. Don't let the thrill of underage drinking rob you of this privilege. Drinking at a young age causes more harm than good. My underage drinking resulted in fights, getting arrested, and all kinds of other drama that lasted long after the parties were over.

PILLS

Pills of any kind, even when prescribed by a doctor, can be harmful to you. There is an enormous problem in our world right now with opioid abuse. It often starts with an injury to your body. If you break your leg, break an arm, or hurt your back, a doctor may prescribe pain medication. These medicines are highly addictive and have many side effects. Addiction to pain medication leads people to try deadlier drugs.

If you suffer from a medical condition, a doctor may prescribe a medicine to help ease the symptoms. If you are under a doctor's care and take your medication as prescribed, it should help you. If this medicine is not working or doing what you expected, stop taking it, and talk to the doctor about other options. Never take more medication than what the doctor prescribed. Any medication can hurt you when not taken correctly.

Never take anyone else's medicine. Taking someone else's medication can literally kill you. Medications often don't mix with certain health conditions or any other medications you may be taking. Mixing medicines can be deadly. Your friend may take it with no problems, but that doesn't mean it will be the same case for you. No short-term high is worth risking your life.

LONG-TERM EFFECTS

Party drugs come in many forms, most of which can be deadly when taken. It's important for you to resist the temptation of wanting to fit in by doing things you're not sure of at this young age. Your brain isn't fully developed until you're twenty-five years old. All drugs and alcohol can have lasting effects on your ability to learn and grow as a person.

Once you become addicted to any substance, it can be extremely difficult to stop using it. Having the willpower and self-dicipline to avoid it now will save you from the struggle of quitting later and the possibility of needing a long-term rehab program to help. If it were easy to quit, most of these programs wouldn't exist. The key is to avoid using these illegal substances now so that you will have a better chance of living longer and having a much more enjoyable life. Remember, just because something is legal doesn't mean it's okay to use it. Just so you know, smoking is probably one of the hardest addictions to kick.

DRIVING UNDER THE INFLUENCE

Not only are drugs and alcohol bad for you in many ways, the consequences of driving under the influence can not only be disastrous but deadly. I can't stress this enough to never drive any type of motorized vehicle while under the influence of drugs or alcohol. By choosing to drive under the influence you are choosing to not only risk your own life but the lives of anyone in your vehicle or anyone you drive by. Don't take that chance.

If you are a passenger, you should never get into a car with anyone who will be driving under the influence. Even if a person tells you he or she has had only had a couple of drinks and is fine, don't do it. There are so many other options now. With ride-share services and cell phones, you can get a ride almost anywhere at any time.

Don't put your life in the hands of someone under the influence of drugs or alcohol. Don't become a victim of someone else's poor judgement. Be smart and make the unpopular decision when necessary to save your own life.

TROUBLE WILL FOLLOW YOU

Drugs and alcohol are a sure way to get you in trouble. Looking back on all the trouble I got into, I now see the pattern. I realize I was never one-hundred-percent sober when I got in trouble. I always had drugs or alcohol in my system when I got arrested. When I think about how I could have avoided all this trouble by not using drugs and alcohol, it frustrates me. My behavior was heavily influenced by the use of illegal substances.

When you're under the influence of any form of drugs or alcohol, your state of mind is altered. You're not able to think as clearly as you would be if you were sober. I cannot stress this point to you enough. You don't want to learn this lesson the hard way, or not be around to tell your story later.

AVOID THE TEMPTATION

In my experience, the best way to stop doing something is to avoid the people, places, and things that make you think about doing drugs or drinking alcohol. Changing your environment is the most effective technique I have ever used when trying to quit something. This applies to anything you want to stop doing.

Certain places may remind you of the thing you are trying to avoid most. It can be difficult to say no to something you may like, but if you know it's wrong or bad for you, do what's best and avoid the temptation. The best way to avoid temptation is to stay away from the people, places, and things that tempt you.

I struggled over the years to quit doing different things. It took a lot of sacrifices to walk away from those people I had fun with and the places where I enjoyed going. Although it was difficult, avoiding the things I knew were bad for me has been worth it. I am now able to live a life where I don't have to worry about waking up in a jail cell or hospital bed. Avoiding temptation is the one thing that worked best for me, and I believe it can also work for you.

TREATMENT OR COUNSELING

If you're using drugs or alcohol and are having trouble quitting on your own, I encourage you to seek professional treatment or some form of help. There are so many programs available to assist you. There is no shame in asking for help. By voluntarily seeking the help you need now, it can prevent personal and legal problems in the future.

If a judge has to force you into a rehabilitation program and it becomes mandatory, you not only lose control of your own life, but it will cost you a lot of money and time you can't get back. Making smart decisions today will help ensure you have a better life tomorrow.

Disclaimer: This is not medical advice; I am not a licensed counselor or doctor. This information is based on my personal experiences and techniques I have used to help myself over the years.

CHAPTER 9

THE PRICE OF TROUBLE

I f you haven't been in any real trouble yet, try your hardest to keep it that way. Trouble comes in many forms. There is minor trouble, like not cleaning your room or doing your homework. These forms of trouble are typical for teens and are not the main focus of this chapter. I'll be talking about serious trouble caused by bad behavior and breaking the law.

BEHAVIORAL PROBLEMS

Bad behavior in school is something you can control. If you have already been in trouble at school or have been suspended at least once in your life, take it as a warning sign of more trouble ahead. In this chapter, I hope to help you identify actual behavioral problems—things that start with fighting, stealing, or skipping class—which can develop into trouble outside of school and eventually lead to you getting arrested.

I mentioned to you briefly earlier in this book about my experience with getting in trouble in school. My issues started showing up around the fifth grade, and because I ignored the warning signs, I went on to have bigger problems. It doesn't matter when these issues start. It's paying attention to them once they do, that's most important. You'll be on a path to more trouble if you don't address these issues right away.

If you're the one causing trouble, you can stop this behavior. If others are negatively influencing you, stop spending time with them. Once you determine what's causing you to misbehave, it'll be easier to avoid the situations that cause it.

By developing respect for your teachers, adults, and the authority figures in your life, it will make it easier for you to treat them better. Being disrespectful is a behavior issue and can create many unnecessary problems in your life. One of the biggest reasons I've seen people act disrespectfully toward others is because they're showing off for their friends. If this is the case for you, stop worrying about what other people think of you, and focus on becoming a more respectful person. You'll get more attention, and for the right reasons.

KNOWING THE DIFFERENCE BETWEEN RIGHT AND WRONG

Because someone doesn't see you doing something wrong, it doesn't make it okay. Knowing right from wrong can be one of your best qualities. Doing what is right or wrong shouldn't depend on who is around you. Make it a habit to always do the right thing.

If you pay attention, the feeling you get when you're doing something right will become familiar to you. In contrast, you may notice a different feeling when doing something wrong. I'm sure you've heard someone say he felt bad when he did something that he knew wasn't right. This feeling is what I am referring to.

If you're getting ready to take something that doesn't belong to you, this may cause a negative feeling, indicating you're not doing the right thing. If this happens, you can stop right where you are, put the item back, and walk away feeling good about yourself.

If you take something and get caught, own up to it, and apologize. Lying to someone's face is disrespectful. It is also insulting their intelligence and a sure way to lose someone's respect and any mercy they might be willing to show you.

Taking things that don't belong to you can lead to a life of crime. If this behavior has tempted you in the past, you know it's wrong, and it's a habit you can break. I mention trouble throughout this book because it has been the one consistent factor associated with all the setbacks in my life. There are some things in life you can't control; getting yourself into trouble isn't one of them.

THE COSTS ASSOCIATED WITH TROUBLE

Getting in trouble can be very expensive. It can lead to hiring lawyers, paying for bail money, and paying fines. Taking time off work and losing money to go to court is also an added expense. It will be especially challenging and inconvenient for your parent or guardian, who will take time off work to bail you out or go to court with you.

The adult in your life is the one who carries the burden and the expense associated with your troubled behavior. Your irresponsible actions can also create friction with your parent and can damage your relationship with him or her. You may also find yourself in a situation where the adult in your life doesn't have the money to bail you out of jail, which means you'll be forced to stay there until someone comes up with the money to get you out.

Being in a juvenile detention facility is no fun, even if it's only for a couple of days. If your bail is less than a thousand dollars, and your parents can't afford to pay it, you'll be stuck there longer. There is nothing worse than the feeling of knowing your freedom only costs a few hundred dollars, and you can't afford it. This could put your parent into a situation where he or she has to choose between paying rent on your house or getting you out of trouble. It places your parent in a very difficult position, and each time something like this happens, it could destroy another piece of your relationship with that parent.

You may also have the added expense of hiring a lawyer. The average criminal defense attorney charges hundreds of dollars per hour. When you're in a low-income situation, and not able to hire a lawyer, you could be assigned a public defender. Depending on your charges, without a good lawyer, you could get a much stiffer sentence from a judge.

This is one of the main reasons the prison system is overflowing with people charged with petty crimes. Have you ever noticed the rich people with serious criminal charges who walk away with little to no consequences? It's because they can afford an excellent lawyer.

Even if you have money, it doesn't automatically get you out of trouble. Sometimes a judge will want to make an example of you. Keep in mind that every time you stand in front of a judge, it's like rolling dice. You never really know what will happen until the gavel drops.

BEING FORCED TO GO TO SCHOOL

In traditional high school, after skipping too many classes and being arrested a few times, a judge sentenced me to a court-appointed high school, which was an all-boys school full of convicted criminals. Because it was court-ordered, had I not gone, I would have been sent directly into a juvenile placement program.

The silver lining for me was that school became the only way for me to get out of my house. Besides being sentenced to the court-appointed school, I was also sentenced to house arrest with an electronic ankle monitor on my leg. The only time I was allowed to leave my house was to go to school, and for the next eleven months, I showed up every day.

Because of attending this court-appointed school every day, I graduated with a high school diploma and a certificate in building maintenance at the age of seventeen. It was a vocational school which taught me carpentry skills I have used throughout my life to earn a living.

Unfortunately for me, I didn't learn the lesson of avoiding the negative people and places in my life. Being surrounded by criminals all day had fueled my bad behavior. I couldn't shake off the street mentality, and within six months of graduating high school, I had accumulated new criminal charges.

DOING TIME

These new charges against me led a judge to sentence me to a juvenile placement program one month before my eighteenth birthday. The courts wanted to certify me as an adult and put me in adult prison because I was so close to being eighteen. However, I was able to keep the case in juvenile court and was sentenced to twelve to thirty-six months in a juvenile program.

Before being placed in a program, I spent several months in a holding facility, The Youth Study Center, in Philadelphia, waiting to find out exactly where I would be serving my time.

Because of my age and the length of my criminal record, my options were limited. It came down to two possibilities—a maximum-security juvenile facility in the suburbs of Philly, or a program called Vision Quest. The people who were locked up in the holding facility with me told horror stories about how bad Vision Quest was and how the staff would assault you if you acted out. They suggested that I should sabotage my interview to avoid going there.

Thankfully, I was smart enough not to take their advice. Sometimes you need to decide for yourself, and I would not let a bunch of strangers dictate where I would do my time. After interviewing with Vision Quest, I knew it would be a better option for me.

I was accepted into the Vision Quest program, and after being there for a while, I realized good behavior was the only thing that would get me out faster. I had some physical altercations in the beginning, and then the counselors explained to me what I would need to do to get out in the minimum amount of time. Then I was able to focus on avoiding any additional trouble and was released in twelve months. I wish I would have spent my teenage years differently.

You can avoid all forms of trouble by becoming the best version of yourself right now. Be a leader, not a follower. By the time you finish this book, you will understand what you need to do to take control of your life. Watch out for those who are looking to drag you down.

GUILTY BY ASSOCIATION

When you spend time with people who are always getting into trouble, you may become guilty by association. The more time you spend with these types of people, the more likely you will find yourself in the wrong place at the wrong time. Avoiding these situations is something else you can take personal responsibility for since you can choose your friends. I have been the victim of guilt by association several times in my life.

When you're with the wrong kind of people all the time, you'll be looked at the same way they are. It's a natural assumption. I should never have gone back to the same environment after getting out of Vision Quest. Going straight back to the same friends and the same neighborhood was the biggest mistake I could have made.

This bad decision is the reason I was put in jail for a few weeks after only being home from Vision Quest for one month. My friends got into a fight with guys from another neighborhood. I wasn't even there, but the people who were assaulted assumed I was because they knew we were close friends. As a result, I got two years' probation, and the people who actually did it got nothing.

Be extra careful who you choose to associate yourself with. If you're spending your time with a bunch of troublemakers, it's only a matter of time before you'll get in trouble too. Enjoy your teenage years, but avoid spending time doing things that will harm your future.

GETTING OUT OF THE SYSTEM IS HARD WORK

Once you get into the criminal justice system, it can be hard to get out. Therefore, it's crucial for you to avoid it at all costs. If you have already been placed into the system, work hard to get out as soon as possible. If you are on probation, follow the rules, complete the punishment, and never look back. It is important to avoid getting into any more trouble that would cause you to get arrested again. If all this sounds foreign to you, that's great. It means you haven't been in serious trouble yet. Please try your best to keep it that way.

HAVING A CRIMINAL RECORD

My criminal record has hurt me throughout my life. If I could go back and do it all over, I would change all of it. Unfortunately for me, or anyone, we cannot go back in time and change the reality of what was. The only thing I can do now is to try and help you avoid going down the same path.

Having a criminal record can affect your life in more ways than you can imagine. Well into the future, when you have changed your life for the better, your criminal history can still hurt you when you are least expecting it. It can cause you to lose job opportunities and hinder you from future successes. Don't let trouble now ruin your future. You can control your behavior, so don't let peer pressure get the best of you. Do what is right for you and your family. Your troubles become the troubles of everyone around you. Don't become a victim and get trapped in the system.

FORCED COUNSELING AND TREATMENT

The entire time I was in the Vision Quest program, I participated in mandatory drug and alcohol rehabilitation treatment, along with a grief and loss group. These groups helped me in ways I had never experienced before. Until going into this program, I had never gone through any formal counseling for either of these issues.

The grief and loss counseling was because the courts knew I had lost both of my parents. This counseling helped me understand more about how to deal with the anger and grief I was experiencing from those losses. Twelve months of consistent counseling gave me an opportunity for healing.

The drug and alcohol counseling I received was also helpful. I learned that most of my troubles had resulted from a lack of caring about myself and always being in an altered state of mind. Using drugs and alcohol negatively affected my outlook on life and my daily actions.

I had already been at a disadvantage in my early years, and I now realize how I made my situation worse through my own poor choices and decisions. I could have avoided all the trouble I have endured in my life if I had known what I am trying to share with you now. Please learn from my mistakes. You deserve better. I hope this book will serve as a guide to a trouble-free life for you.

CHAPTER 10

DEVELOPING YOUR CHARACTER

Your character on the inside will show on the outside. People will judge you based on your actions, the way you carry yourself, and the way you treat other people. Your actions come from your belief system. If you believe you're a good person, you'll act like one. You can become a better version of yourself by making some slight adjustments.

I'm sharing with you the things I've done over the past fourteen years to improve the quality of my life. As a street kid with a bad attitude, there was a lot I needed to change about myself to become a better person. When I became aware of self-help and personal development information, it changed my life. The things you're about to read are the fundamentals of changing your self-image.

DEVELOPING YOUR CHARACTER

Reading, watching, and listening to positive and inspirational information will help to develop your character. This process is something you will want to continue throughout your life as you grow as a person. You have already started building the foundation by reading this book. As you implement what you're learning, you're improving yourself and becoming a better person with every action you take.

By self-educating yourself on how to improve your self-image, and implementing what you're learning, your outlook on life will begin to change. People will notice your growth, and you'll feel better too. You can't just read one book and think that's enough. Make it a habit to seek out new ways to improve yourself every day. Consistency is the key to developing long-lasting, positive changes.

ALWAYS BE TRUTHFUL — NOBODY TRUSTS A LIAR

Being a truthful person starts by being honest with yourself first. Accept who you are. Being truthful with yourself is recognizing where you are and where you could use some improvement. You may try to convince yourself you're better at something than you are. You may want to achieve a specific goal but procrastinate by telling yourself you'll do it later, and it never gets done.

When you tell yourself you want to do a specific thing, make it your mission to get it done. Don't lie to yourself and make excuses for why you're not finding the time to do what's important to you. If it's really important, you have to make time. Making excuses and accepting them is a form of lying to yourself.

Being truthful with other people will help to develop your character. Truthfulness means being honest with someone even when you've made a mistake. People appreciate honesty, even when the news isn't pleasant. Once someone catches you in a lie, it will be hard for that person to trust you again.

He or she might not call you out on the lie, which may lead you to believe you got away with it. Some people dislike conflict and would rather just let it go than confront you. Soon that person may begin to avoid being around you because he or she thinks they can no longer believe what you say.

If people have to analyze everything you say, they may just decide you're not worth their time. If you become known as a liar, word will get around to all your friends. Once word spreads, you'll start to notice the difference in how people see you and treat you. As I said, they may not call you out on it to your face, but they will identify you as a liar to other people.

This one simple behavior will have a negative effect on you in school, in social circles, and in a job environment. People will talk about you behind your back, and you will become known as someone who can't be trusted. Once you become known as a liar, even when you tell the truth, no one will believe you. Even if what you have to say will make you look bad, it's still better, to be honest, and look bad than it is to get caught in a lie. Remembering the truth is much easier than remembering a lie. If you tell a lie about something and the subject comes back up in a later conversation, you likely won't remember exactly what you said. You'll then create a different lie that may become a totally different story. This is when you'll get caught.

Make it a habit to always tell the truth, and you won't have anything to worry about or any reason to feel guilty. Lying is a habit you can break right now if you are already doing it. You can decide today to no longer tell lies or to ever start.

MANNERS AND RESPECT

Respecting people is an important part of developing good character. Showing respect to other people is how you will gain their respect in return. This means respecting people, even when no one else is around to see it. Do it because you want to and not because someone is making you.

Your manners will have a significant effect on the way people see you. Having good manners is another essential part of building good character. Saying please and thank you should become second nature. Making a habit of doing this now will stay with you forever and be an example for those people closest to you.

People will notice your good manners, and it will help them see you in a positive way. Saying please and thank you are the basics. Saying bless you to someone who sneezes and excuse me when you burp in public or when you walk in front of someone in your path are also signs of good manners. Excuse me is one of the core manners you should exercise daily.

Opening a door and holding one open for someone are also ways of showing good manners. Another one is saying you're sorry when it's necessary. Be sure to apologize when you do something that needs an apology. If you practice this regularly, you'll begin to do it without having to think about it.

LEARN TO TRUST YOURSELF AND OTHER PEOPLE

Trusting in yourself and others will help you develop character. When people know they can trust you, they will tell other people how trustworthy you are. Having a reputation for being trustworthy can go a long way in life.

It's essential to have people trust you because once you gain someone's trust, you can build on it. When people trust you, they will be comfortable referring you to others for jobs, which is very important in obtaining employment. Having people trust you is a key to advancement, not only in your character but in your life.

Trust is tied, in part, to lying. If you're a liar, people won't trust you. Another way of developing your character is by becoming a truthful person. I'm sure you're beginning to see a pattern here—how all the things I'm talking about are connected.

There are many parts of your character over which you have total control. The way you see yourself is an essential part of the way other people will see you. Therefore, it will be beneficial for you to develop self-confidence. You must trust yourself and your instincts. This is what should guide your actions and the way you think about yourself.

When you're comfortable in knowing what you're doing is right, be careful about letting outside forces change your mind. Getting to know yourself can be one of the most powerful things you can do. Having faith in yourself will help you trust your decisions and judgement. When you believe in yourself and trust yourself, you will become more confident in your choices.

YOUR BEHAVIOR CAN DEFINE YOU

Do you pick on or make fun of other people? Accepting people for who they are is an especially important aspect of your character. Bullying people is disrespectful. If someone is doing this to you, one of the best ways to handle it is to ignore them and walk away. That bully will find someone else to pick on. People will have a hard time respecting you when they see you disrespecting others.

Bullying may seem like the cool thing to do when you're showing off for your friends, but it's not helping to build up your character. Be kind, courteous, and respectful to everyone you meet, regardless of who they are. You may not realize who a certain person is until long after you have met them for the first time.

Do you want to be known as a troublemaker? I would hope not. As you're positively developing your character, your behavior on the outside will reflect it. These behaviors happen without you even realizing it. Improving yourself is something you should aspire to do throughout your entire life.

Continuing to learn and grow as a person will ensure you're always becoming a better version of yourself. Become consistent in your growth, and people will notice. If you're improving yourself all week and then on the weekend you hang out on the street corner cursing and disrespecting others, it will sabotage the progress you're making. Make this a full-time commitment, and the rewards will be endless.

CREATING AN ATTRACTIVE PERSONALITY

Taking action and implementing these things I've talked about will ensure you are creating an attractive personality. People will want to spend more time with you. They may want to know what you're doing because your positivity will become contagious.

Working to become the best version of yourself is your way of controlling your future. Try not to dwell on your past. Focus on how much more amazing you can become instead. You have greatness inside you. Bring it out.

Be authentic, be unique, and be true to yourself. Don't be fake or try to do things only to impress other people. I will cover more self-development strategies in the last chapter of this book. Congratulations on getting this far. Keep up the excellent work and continue to read on.

CHAPTER 11

BECOMING AWARE OF YOUR HABITS

Willpower is a strong character trait that will help you resist temptations and give you the strength to keep going when times get tough. Studies show it takes a minimum of twenty-one consecutive days of doing something to develop a habit. They also suggest it takes a minimum of twenty-one days of not doing something to break a habit.

The quality of your habits can determine the quality of your life. Your goal should be to limit the number of bad habits you have and maximize the amount of good habits you have.

WHERE TO START

You could begin with the way you take care of yourself, like creating the habit of healthy eating and daily exercise. Making your bed, brushing your teeth, and putting on deodorant and clean clothes consistently every morning will become good habits in your morning routine. This is basic stuff. It shouldn't require an adult to make you do these things.

Habits take time to start and can be hard to break. Be careful of the negative things you consistently do. Keep this in mind and look at things you have been doing for a long time. Are there things you do that you're not happy about and would like to change?

Do you have a habit of biting your nails when you get nervous? Do you have a habit of chewing on pens and pencils in school? Even simple practices like these can be causing damage you're not aware of. For example, biting your nails can cause infections in your mouth from bacteria, and chewing on things other than food can cause damage to your teeth.

Strategies to improve your self-image and self-worth are good habits you can start implementing right away. Start small by replacing habits one by one. Try to get to the point where the positives outweigh the negatives. If this is all new to you, be patient, and believe you can do it.

EXAMPLES OF SOME GOOD HABITS

Doing your schoolwork or homework without having to be told, getting up early, and developing a healthy morning routine are all good habits. The habit of coming home from school, having a snack, and watching TV for a little while before getting into your homework is perfectly fine. However, if you spend two hours watching TV and must be told to do your homework, this could be a bad habit.

Take the initiative and get your schoolwork done before you kick back and relax for the night. Make it a habit to avoid doing everything at the last minute, like doing homework on your way to school. Being prepared is a valuable life skill and is a behavior you can control. You are young, use your energy, and avoid becoming lazy.

Give yourself extra time in the morning. After making your bed, you can use this time to read a few pages of a book or relax and think about how you want your day to go. You could also do some jumping jacks, sit-ups, or pushups in your bedroom before you get into the shower. After finishing your quick exercise routine, you can eat a healthy breakfast, like some eggs and bacon, as opposed to a quick bowl of sugary cereal.

Getting up early in the morning prevents you from rushing out the door without taking proper care of yourself. If you wake up five minutes before the bus comes, you won't have time to do the very basics. You may rush out the door, forgetting to brush your teeth, putting on clothes that may stink, and going hungry until lunchtime. When you don't eat a nutritious breakfast, you could have low energy, which can cause you to be miserable and make it hard to concentrate. Give these things a try before making a judgement about whether they will work for you or not.

EXAMPLES OF SOME BAD HABITS

Not cleaning up after yourself, leaving messes all around the house, being disrespectful to the people you live with, and not following the house rules, are just a few examples. Having a negative attitude, not accepting personal responsibility, and always blaming other people are all habits you can change. Think of the areas of your life where you know you can improve.

You could also develop the negative habits of smoking or drinking alcohol. I want you to realize these habits, if you have them, will hurt you and the quality of your life. You can be an energetic, carefree teenager without this negativity. By depending on substances to support your mood, you are limiting your ability to be happy and healthy.

Skipping classes or whole days of school is a negative habit you should avoid. Getting an education is one of the most important things you can do as a young person. Now is not the time in your life to be focused on partying and wasting time. Even if some school days may be boring and torturous, hang in there, and take care of business. School is your job as a teenager.

KNOWING WHAT TO WATCH OUT FOR

Take a step back and look at the way you have been living. Can you see where some things you have been doing could be negatively affecting your life? If you don't have any of the negative habits I've mentioned here in this chapter or book, that's great. You need to know what to look out for, so if negative patterns show up, you can stop them right away.

Some of this stuff may not make sense to you if you're younger. As you get older, these types of things could start to appear in your life. If they do, I hope what I've brought to your attention in this book will help you recognize these patterns before they become bad habits. Developing negative habits could happen before you know it if you're not paying attention.

BE PATIENT WITH YOURSELF

Once you develop a habit, it can stay with you for the rest of your life, so be careful what habits you're creating. This will require discipline, but you control what habits you practice. Be patient with yourself, and don't get frustrated. If you have a full week of doing something positive and then have a bad day, start again fresh the next day. Being consistent is important, but if you miss one day, don't beat yourself up over it. Refocus and start again right away.

You are young, and time is on your side. It may take a few months to develop new habits and break your old ones, but the time invested will be well worth it. Create a personal initiative to achieve your goals of creating and breaking habits.

I understand you may have no one around to tell you what to do or how to do it. The goal of this book is to provide you with the knowledge of what you can do and how you can do it on your own if necessary.

Sometimes you may need someone to let you know you're doing an excellent job, give you some recognition, and keep you motivated. If you have a person in your life who is supportive, I suggest you let that person know of your intention to create a better version of yourself. Then ask for his or her support and encouragement. Having a support system can also provide accountability, which can help keep you focused on your goals.

Visit www.TheSelfHelpCompany.com for information to help support you along your journey of personal discovery and self-improvement. Please join my mailing list for emails about new and updated content coming out all the time. Subscribe to my podcast, social media pages, video pages, and read my blog for more information related to the topics in this book and more.

CHAPTER 12

TAKING CARE OF YOURSELF

The basics of taking care of yourself go beyond what I discussed in the chapter on physical well-being. If you are already practicing those positive habits, keep up the good work. This chapter includes more information about essential life skills that could shape your future.

PERSONAL HYGIENE

It's very important to shower and apply deodorant daily. Your body is changing, and you're sweating more. So, if you don't do this, you'll have body odor, which is not the kind of attention you want to draw to yourself. The same thing applies when brushing your teeth. Stinky breath is a sure way to keep people away from you.

Staying clean and well-groomed are basic everyday habits you should implement if you are not already doing so.

KEEPING YOUR CLOTHES CLEAN

If you wear the same clothes for days in a row, they'll begin to smell bad. You may not notice it, but other people will. This includes hoodies, which you may have a habit of wearing for weeks without washing them. You should always put on clean clothes every day.

Be sure to iron your clothes. They may be clean, but if they have a lot of wrinkles, they'll look like you pulled them out of the dirty clothes hamper. Take the time to iron your clothes so they look presentable. A trick you can use is to put the wrinkled clothes into the dryer for a couple of minutes. Doing this will help get wrinkles out.

Speaking of the dryer, let's talk about learning how to do your laundry. This is an essential life skill you need to become a responsible adult. You may have the luxury of having someone else who does your laundry right now, but this will not always be the case. Take the initiative and ask someone to teach you how to do it. Learning this task will prepare you to live on your own.

Helping around the house will show the adult in your life that you are responsible. Doing your laundry, keeping the dirty clothes off your floor, and keeping your room clean will not only make them happy but might even result in you getting some allowance money.

KNOWING YOUR WAY AROUND THE KITCHEN

Learn how to cook basic meals for yourself. There are many appliances in the kitchen, some big and some small. Nobody wants you to burn the house down, so ask someone to show you how to use the appliances safely.

There is a stove that may have flames on the top. There are specific ways to work with these to avoid burning yourself or something else. Learning how to cook on the stovetop is essential for being able to feed yourself healthy foods. These skills will give you the ability to live on your own once you know how to cook for yourself, do your laundry, and clean.

There are also smaller appliances in your kitchen, such as the toaster, microwave, blender, and can opener. There may be others, but these are the basics, and you should know how to use them all. If you become the man or woman of the house, knowing how to do the basics is essential.

For example, if your parent gets hurt and can't take care of himself or herself, you may need to step up and help without much notice. Your parent can't show you how to do these things if he or she is sick or in bed and can't get up. Be prepared for the unexpected. If something were to happen to the person who takes care of you, would you be able to take care of yourself right now?

Learning how to cook basic meals, such as eggs, hot dogs, spaghetti, and grilled cheese sandwiches are easy skills to learn. You cannot live on bowls of cereal forever. You can get recipe books and take cooking lessons by watching YouTube videos and learn in a couple of hours how to do the basics. Don't make excuses. Understand the value of knowing how to do these things for yourself.

Once you have finished cooking, there will almost always be a mess to clean up. Be responsible and clean up after yourself, especially in the kitchen. Leaving food messes lying around can cause bacteria to build up, which can make you sick. Cleaning the countertops after preparing food is easy to do and only takes a minute. You should also make it a habit to take the trash out when the bag gets full. Do what you can to keep your house from developing foul odors. Be sure to learn how to wash the dishes properly. Keeping the kitchen clean is just the beginning of learning how to clean and manage on your own.

CLEANING

Using the vacuum cleaner is something you should know how to do. Vacuuming includes moving furniture and other stuff out of the way, so you do a thorough job and don't miss anything. Pick up any big things off the floor first, and be careful not to run over something that could break the vacuum cleaner.

Other areas may require you to use a broom to sweep up the dirt and a dustpan and brush to pick it up. You always want to sweep up loose dirt before using a mop. Sweeping first will save you much aggravation. Mopping the floors is an essential part of keeping your house clean. This includes your bathrooms and all other hard surfaces like wood and tile.

Make it a habit to clean your bathroom regularly, including wiping down your sink and toilet with some form of disinfectant.

Keeping your bathroom clean will help avoid the buildup of bacteria and germs that can cause you to get sick.

Cleaning is often part of weekly chores. Try not to make people ask you multiple times to do these things. Doing your chores should be something you get excited about because it's teaching you the necessary life skills for when you become an adult and live on your own.

SHARING SPACE WITH OTHERS

There could come a time in life where you may live with a roommate. Having your own apartment or house is a great accomplishment. When something is yours, you will learn to appreciate it much more. Keeping your space clean will make you feel so proud.

How would you feel if your roommate left a mess everywhere? Being a messy roommate could cause you to have fights and arguments amongst your roommates. If this becomes the case, they may ask you to move out. Being asked to move out because of dirty habits can be embarrassing. You would have to find a new place to live, which is difficult, especially with brief notice.

LEARNING THE HARD WAY

As a kid, I didn't have many of the skills I've shared with you in this chapter. My mom did most of these basic things for me. Having someone do stuff for you is nice, but it doesn't teach you anything. As I got older, when my mom would be at work, I had to keep it simple with peanut butter and jelly sandwiches and bowls of cereal because I had no cooking skills.

When my mom was sick, and in the hospital, my brother and I lived alone in our house. Because we didn't have many of these life skills, we didn't do any food shopping, and only cooked in the microwave. We mostly survived by ordering pizza. The house was always a mess, and I can't remember doing any cleaning or laundry.

One of the last things I had to do before getting released from the Vision Quest program was to spend one month in a group home. I lived in a house full of teenagers with staff supervision, learning all the necessary skills I just mentioned to you. We had to go to a laundromat and do our own laundry, learn to cook basic meals, and clean the house in all the ways I just shared with you.

Being forced to live in a house full of strangers was not an ideal way to learn these things, but it worked. I hope you now see the value of knowing these things and learning them on your own terms.

If you want to be seen as a mature and responsible teenager, learning and practicing these skills will help you achieve that goal. These are skills that will last you a lifetime. Develop these good habits now, and you will earn a sense of independence and pride.

CHAPTER 13

Hobbies and Ways to Spend Your Time

If money was not an issue, what would you do with your time? If you could choose any profession in the world but not get paid to do it, what would it be? The answer to these questions will help you discover your passions. This chapter is about helping you identify what motivates you. My goal is to help you find ways to add fun, laughter, and excitement into your life.

DISCOVERING YOUR PASSION

Figuring out what you're most passionate about is the best place to start when choosing your hobbies. There are thousands of things you can do as a hobby. The ones I will mention are just to get your juices flowing and your creative wheels turning. When other ideas pop into your head as you read this chapter, write them down.

PLAYING SPORTS

There are many sports in which you could participate. You could start with one you enjoy watching other people play. You can learn something new or consider a sport you may have played when you were younger. Is there something you enjoyed as a kid that you could start doing again? This idea does not only have to be associated with sports.

The valuable thing about almost any sport is teamwork. A close-knit team can become like a family environment. Being involved in sports is an aspect of socializing, even if you are only a team of two, and it will give you more opportunities to interact with new people.

Another valuable thing about sports is what you can learn from a coach. You can always learn something from someone with more experience, and you can benefit from a coach's advice in many areas of your life. Even if you have a natural talent for a particular sport, a coach can help improve your skills.

LEARNING TO PLAY AN INSTRUMENT

Like sports, there are many instruments you can learn to play. Depending on your interest, you can choose from a small instrument, like a harmonica, to bigger instruments, like drums or a piano. Music is a way to create something from nothing. This creativity can give you a sense of accomplishment and skills which could provide more opportunities for you.

If you develop a genuine passion for an instrument or several instruments and stick with it, you could become a professional musician. Many musicians can play every instrument on the stage. The more instruments you can play, the more valuable you become.

Your ability to feel valuable creates a sense of worth, which you might not have felt in a while. This new hobby could also take attention away from negativity going on in your life and give you a sense of purpose.

Playing an instrument requires you to listen to the music of the genre you are learning to play. Listening to music is also a powerful healing tool. Finding music that will calm you and put your mind at ease can be helpful. Listening to angry music with negative lyrics can bring your mood down. Focusing on upbeat music can lift your spirits and create positive vibes in your mind.

PHOTOGRAPHY

Photography can be an exciting skill to learn. We can all take regular pictures with the cameras on our phones, but becoming an expert photographer is a learned skill. If you enjoy taking photos, this can be a great hobby. You could get a good camera and take beautiful pictures people would buy.

Being able to focus on a single image, such as beautiful scenery or people with significant expressions, can be inspiring and healing. This can provide a positive outlet and stimulate your creativity by learning more about how photography works.

If this topic excites you, start by taking baby steps toward learning the craft. If you focus on this and study it long enough, you could become a professional. As technology evolves, so do the cameras which are available. You could learn the history of the camera and different techniques used to develop pictures over the years. Photography is a hobby with many benefits. Finding beautiful locations you want to photograph leads us to our next hobby idea.

TRAVEL WHEN YOU CAN

You may not have total control over this now. But if you show excitement about wanting to discover new locations, you could share this excitement with the adults in your life, and they just might agree to take you. Take the time to research places you might like to visit. Learn the history and landmarks of local towns and cities nearby. You could start with family vacation ideas.

Make a separate list of places you would like to visit when you become an adult and can travel on your own. You may be inspired to travel the world someday. Start locally and add to your list as you learn about new and exciting places. This dream will give you something to look forward to and help you create a vision of where you want to go in the future. Don't forget to take lots of pictures!

RIDING A BIKE

You can ride a bicycle for pleasure, or you could ride for sport. If you don't own a pedal bike or don't know how to ride one, this could be a new hobby for you to try. If you have a fear of doing this, start small and ask somebody to help you.

I know what you're thinking, *riding a bike is boring*. That doesn't have to be the case. You can make it exciting based on where you ride. Riding around your neighborhood may not be very thrilling but consider the idea of mountain biking through a national park with beautiful scenery, lakes, and monuments. Being surrounded by nature can give you a genuine sense of freedom.

Riding a bike can become a professional hobby if you choose. If you watch action sports, you'll see there are different ways people ride pedal bikes. You could do tricks, ride for speed, or a little of both, and become a racer. Racing incorporates speed, jumping, and other forms of daring feats that can increase the adventure.

If you already have some basic experience, learn how to take your skills to the next level. Biking can be an excellent form of exercise and a great way to get you active and make new friends.

SKATEBOARDING OR SURFING

Riding a skateboard requires balance, and it's a great way to create self-discipline. Once you can balance yourself on a skateboard, you could balance yourself on a surfboard too. You may notice that some skaters also surf. If you are fortunate enough to live near an ocean, maybe surfing could be your thing. Skateboarding is another way of expressing your creativity.

You could learn tricks and find ways to express yourself. Skating is also something you can do socially. Visiting skate parks will allow you to engage with people who also enjoy the same things as you, and it can be a fun hobby to get excited about. Finding something you have in common with other people is easy to do. You just need to make an effort to find them.

COMMON INTERESTS

Finding hobbies and common interests with your family members can be valuable in maintaining good family relationships. Finding something everyone likes and can do together will create bonding opportunities and help you get to know each other better. Relaxing and having fun can put everyone at ease and allow them to be themselves without all the stress of everyday life.

Try this exercise. Write out all the things you enjoy doing and have your siblings and adults in your life make a list of their own. Once you all have your lists made, compare them, and see if there are any common items. If so, start with the thing everyone likes. Then make a plan to spend time together bonding over the mutual interests you all enjoy. Continuing to look for fresh ways to interact and socialize with your family members will strengthen your relationship in a way you can all enjoy.

This concept can also work with your friends. If you're getting tired of doing the same things all the time, have everyone make a list of their interests. You may discover new stuff about each other and have a whole newfound list of things to do together.

LEARNING A SECOND LANGUAGE

Being able to speak multiple languages can be a valuable life skill. When you can communicate with people from other cultures, it can open doors to new opportunities. You could start by making a list of places you want to visit, research those locations, and find out what local languages they speak there.

For example, if one of your favorite places in the world is Germany and you plan to visit there when you're older, start learning to speak German now. Learning an unfamiliar language takes time and discipline. The sooner you start, the faster you will become fluent.

Knowing how to speak a second language is also an unbelievably valuable skill for job employment. The more languages you know, the more valuable you become in specific job markets.

It is much easier to learn a second language while you're young. You may not be thinking of this as a hobby, but it is a productive and positive way to spend your time. There are many language learning programs available. There are smartphone apps you can use—some requiring only fifteen minutes of practice per day.

STUDYING FOR YOUR FUTURE

A positive way to spend your time now is to study for the future. I'll give you a couple of examples so you can understand what I mean.

You may be too young to get your driver's license right now, but there is no law against how old you need to be to study for the test. Get a copy of the manual and start studying it, so when the time comes, you will be prepared. Most people wait until they are old enough to get the driver's license to study for the test. These people often must take their driving test multiple times because they are unprepared. You can avoid failing on your first try by starting to study now and become an expert on the information you will need to know later.

Another example of this is if you have an interest in a specific job field or career, you could learn more about the industry to better understand what it will take to be successful later. Is making a lot of money when you become an adult, something that interests you? If so, you could begin studying the industries which offer the highest-earning incomes. Once you have identified these industries, you could decide which one interests you most, and then focus in on it.

For example, selling real estate can be a high-paying career. Becoming a real estate agent takes time. It requires a specific type of real estate schooling before you can get a real estate license. I have gone to real estate school and obtained a real estate license. Having to learn a lot of information in a brief amount of time can be stressful.

Before completing real estate school, you must take a test. I failed the school test on my first try. If I had been studying the book before I went to the real estate school, I would have been more prepared. You can start exploring the book now if you choose to. You can get access to this information without having to be enrolled in a real estate school.

There is traditional book knowledge, and then there are industry professionals who share their practical experience through different training programs and books. These experts teach valuable skills not taught in school. Learning this information now will position you to experience success much faster than if you wait until you start a job to learn about it.

After you get a real estate license, you must work with a brokerage firm. You could begin researching brokerage companies in your area, learn more about them, and maybe see who you would want to work with once you can do so.

There are many other industries you can learn more about right now in your spare time if you choose. There is no age limit on studying and learning. You can get books from the library about every way imaginable to make money.

Prepare yourself now for when you are old enough to get a job in your desired field. If you love what you do, you will be much more motivated and excited to do it. Being happy in the career you choose can be worth just as much as the money you earn. It is better to do the research now than it is to just settle for anything later.

Trying new things can be an exciting adventure. Let your imagination guide you. When something interests you, take time to learn more about it. Once you find something that excites you, stick with it. You'll never know if you like something unless you try it.

CHAPTER 14

TECHNOLOGY — MAKE IT WORK FOR YOU

Technology is your friend, but make it your servant, not your master. What I mean by this is, there are positive and negative ways to use technology. Be careful how much time you spend on social media, watching challenge videos, prank videos, or surfing the Internet looking for ways to spend your money. This type of usage is not serving you in the best way.

In this chapter, I will share ideas on how you can use the power of technology to enhance the quality of your life. This information will help shift your mindset from consumer to creator. Are you ready to open your mind to new ways of looking at the Internet, your computer, your phone, and all other electronics you possess?

SOCIAL MEDIA

We all use social media platforms through our smartphones and computers. Social networking has become an essential part of our daily lives. Social media is a powerful way to keep in touch with our friends, but it can also be so much more.

Spending too much time on social media can lead to negativity and drama if you only focus on what friends are saying about each other. If you're always checking your comments and worrying about how many people like your posts, you can become discouraged. You may get into arguments and become self-conscious about what people think of you.

Thinking back to the hobbies chapter, what social networking groups can you join to surround yourself with people who have common interests? I have found writers' groups on Facebook who have provided valuable insights for me as an aspiring writer— knowledge I wouldn't be able to get from friends who have no writing experience. I also use Facebook groups for support when I need to learn how to use software that's new to me. Find groups that will support and encourage you on whatever journey you are taking.

TECHNOLOGY IS THE FUTURE

Try not to take technology for granted. You were born into the digital age and may assume it was always here. I was a teenager in the early 1990s when the Internet was new and nothing compared to what it is today. Computers were huge and very expensive, not to mention powered by a dial-up internet connection, which was extremely slow.

The only way for me to make money as a teenager was to go out and physically earn it through a job. With the technology available to you today, this is no longer the case. Technology is still in its infancy and is developing at a rapid pace. You can take full advantage of the opportunities it presents. Think about virtual reality and artificial intelligence for a minute. Now try to imagine where we will be twenty years from now.

Be creative with the technology you have. Cultivate your creative vision, which is buried inside you somewhere, even if you're not aware of it. We can use the Internet for almost anything these days. Regardless of what your interests are, there's a way to use technology to bring your creative vision to life.

LEARNING THROUGH TECHNOLOGY

You can maximize watching videos by learning from them. It's okay to be entertained, but videos are also a helpful learning resource. Everyone needs a good laugh sometimes, just try to balance the time between entertainment and education.

Watching videos, reading blogs, and listening to podcasts are the new ways of getting a free education in today's world. There is nothing you can't learn through these technology mediums. Once you identify what you're interested in, you can take full advantage of these channels to educate yourself.

There are tons of digital ebook platforms available, offering books on how to do just about anything. You may not always want to read, so there are also audiobooks where you can listen to the book instead of reading it. These are often available in your local library for free.

You don't always need to spend money to gain access to this information. If you have a specific book in mind, even an audiobook, if your local library doesn't have it, you can ask them to order it. It may take a little time, but you can get something similar while you wait.

If you don't own a computer or have internet access, you can go to the local library and use computers there. By spending only a couple of hours a day on a library computer, you can learn anything.

Besides computers and cell phones, there are other forms of technology to consider. Cameras, MP3 players, tablets, virtual reality headsets, drones, and digital voice recorders can all be useful tools. These are forms of technology you may not have considered as a resource for you to learn, grow, and entertain yourself.

YOUR PEERS ARE MAKING MONEY ONLINE

Think about how people are using video platforms to share their ideas with others to create an income. Whether they're recording themselves playing a video game or doing a dance challenge, every time an advertisement plays during the video, that person is making money. If you're not aware, this is the way your favorite YouTuber is making money when you watch his or her videos.

While you're watching and clicking, they're getting paid. Most of these people are just being themselves. They're expressing their creativity and knowledge, and people enjoy watching it. Have you ever been asked to buy something or to click a link in the description?

Another way these social media influencers are getting paid is from their merchandise. Have you ever bought merch from your favorite social media personality? Can you come up with a catchy idea for a t-shirt design? There are t-shirt print-on-demand, dropship companies that will handle all the sales for you and send you a percentage of the profits.

The bigger your following, the more money you can make. You can also get paid from advertisers with products related to your content. Once you realize these things are possible, you'll feel as if you're wasting time when browsing the web with no purpose. Make the time you spend online count. Be intentional with how you spend it.

YOU CAN BECOME THE INFLUENCER

Technology can also become a source of income if you choose. As I mentioned, your favorite YouTuber is making a living by creating videos. Why can't this be you? Do you have a talent or skill people would enjoy watching? You can create videos based on your passions or hobbies.

For example, are you good at playing video games? You can record your screen and teach people how to play better. Some platforms also allow you to broadcast live and build a fan base of people who will show up to see you play.

You can create any type of video. These might be of you talking about your hobbies and interests, or of animated cartoon characters just for fun. Videos can also be a series of informational slides you can narrate to help people learn a specific topic or skill. These videos can be anything from teaching hairstyles to making music. Start making a list of ideas.

Once you learn how to create videos, you can turn them into money. You can have sponsored ads embedded in your video by companies related to your content. The sky's the limit on the type of videos you can make and ways to turn them into money.

You can have your own line of branded merch for sale. You could also become an affiliate of companies who sell products that would interest your audience. I talk more about affiliate programs in the making money chapter. Learning about these things can be an excellent use of your time. If you start now while you're young and get good at it, this can be an enjoyable way to make a living.

You can use video programs to create short commercials for local businesses. Then you could help them set up their own video-streaming channel. There is easy-to-use software you can use to make an animated video with built-in voice-over features. No camera or microphone is needed, you type in words, and the program does the talking. Small businesses in your neighborhood could benefit from you doing this for them. Think about someone who could use this service, like maybe your neighbor, who has a landscaping business.

Creating videos can be easy. There are many free resources to help you make quality videos. Putting them on YouTube and most other video platforms are free. If you have a computer with a camera and a microphone, you have the basic tools needed. If you don't have your own computer with a camera, this may also be something you can do at a library or in a school computer room.

You could ask your teacher for permission to spend your lunch break in the computer lab. Creative thinking is one way to take your life to the next level. There is no excuse for being bored when you have access to these tools and resources at your fingertips.

Some of this may be brand new to you, and some of it you may have only heard about, but hopefully, this will inspire you to make the most of what technology has to offer.

WRITING A BOOK

I am creating this book using a digital recorder to record my voice, and then I'm using a program on my computer to transcribe it into text. Then I use another program to edit that text. There are also different programs I'm using for other parts of the book creation process. Writing a book is no longer somebody sitting at a desk writing with pen and paper.

Yes, there are some small bits of writing by hand, mostly taking notes, but it's very little compared to the old way of doing things. If you have a deep passion or desire for a particular topic, you could write a book about it. Your book can be on any subject or topic you choose. You could create a children's book, a picture book, a journal, a workbook, or even a comic book. Fiction or non-fiction, the possibilities are endless.

This is my first book, and I had a lot to learn. I have invested my time in reading books, watching videos, listening to writers' podcasts, and asking questions of people with experience. I joined a writers' group at my local library where people genuinely wanted to help me. I joined online writing groups with people who share their knowledge and experience regularly.

I had to learn everything I now know to give you this finished product. You can do the same thing. There are many ways you can map out your ideas. There are mind mapping programs to help with brainstorming ideas, and another one I use to help plot out the story.

The process I'm using to create this book is being done almost one hundred percent by using different technologies. From every aspect of creating this book to every part of publishing it, I'm using some form of technology.

You have a story to tell, and you can learn how to write it. Writing can be both healing and profitable at the same time. The story you write doesn't need to be personal; it can be fiction made up from your imagination. Start with writing a short story and see where your creativity takes you.

I'll provide resources on my website with a list of writing tools I use and the places you can self-publish your book. I'll also post a video of me recording and transcribing a small part of this book. Check out www.TheSelfHelpCompany.com/writing-tools

CREATING WEBSITES

Another way to make money by using technology is to learn how to create websites. I know you're probably thinking you don't know-how. I was in your shoes thirteen years ago when I built my first website. I was a full-time construction worker with no computer knowledge, other than sending emails and surfing the web.

When I started with my first home-based business, the company gave me a website. I would provide people with my business card, but I could never tell who was visiting the site. I learned it would be beneficial for me to have my own website with an email address form to track the visitors and get their contact information to be able to follow up with them.

I hired someone to do it for me, but they were taking too long, so I learned how to do it myself. After watching hours of videos and investing in an inexpensive piece of software, I successfully created a website. Once I did it for myself a few times, I became good enough to charge other people to build their websites.

This skill led me to develop an Internet marketing training website where people paid me money to teach them what I had learned. Building a website is something you can do a lot easier than I could thirteen years ago. Now there are website building programs available that allow you to drag and drop, point and click. You could have a website up and running in a matter of hours today. This fact is not an exaggeration, and you can put up a simple site for free through a few companies. Once you can build a website for yourself, you'll know how to do it for others.

Imagine someone paying you to put up a website. Not everyone is tech-savvy. Like your neighbor, who I mentioned earlier, if you make a video commercial for them, you can also make a website for them too. A small business may not be able to afford an expensive company to create a website. You can do it much cheaper, and the business pays for the web tools and you for doing the work.

These are examples of things you can do. Try a few of these ideas and see which ones excite you the most, then focus on them. Think outside the box and continue to come up with new ideas. Believe in yourself and take action. If something doesn't work, learn from your mistakes, and try again.

DEVELOPING MOBILE APPS

I'm sure I don't need to tell you that mobile apps are hot right now. Developing mobile apps is becoming easier every day, and you are the perfect person to take advantage of it. Your knowledge of how apps work gives you an advantage in developing them.

You can learn to code and build them from scratch, or you can use mobile app development websites that give you a plug-and-play system. These are skills you can learn on your own by watching videos and reading books.

If you're looking to take this skill and turn it into a full-time, money-earning job, there are more advanced methods you can use. Consider looking into a STEM program or a technical school that teaches classes on how to learn these different technologies. If you're bored with traditional school, this can be a way for you to get excited about learning. Wouldn't it be great to have fun and develop valuable skills at the same time?

There are many high school and college programs that can prepare you for a high-paying career in technology fields. Look into schools and programs in your area. They may offer classes at your local library. Do your research and become educated on what it will take. Share this information with the supporting adult in your life. You may be able to start sooner than you think.

IF YOU'RE A GAMER

If you enjoy playing video games, consider learning how to create your own game. When you're playing, you may often think that you don't like how the game works, or you wish it had better features. This thought is your creative side coming out. You're envisioning ways to improve the game. If you can see a way to enhance an existing game, it could be possible for you to create something better.

Yes, you may need to learn how to do it, but just like with websites and mobile apps, there are ways you can learn to create video games too. You can learn to code and develop a game from scratch, or you can investigate websites that have templates for you to drag and drop.

Some of these apps will give you the freedom to create characters, build worlds, and develop your ideas using their platform. You can try this out as a hobby, something you do for yourself and your friends. If you enjoy learning these new skills and take it seriously, this could turn into a paying job working for a game company one day.

You can also create a game and sell it to a game company or make it available in the app stores. You could turn your game into a mobile app and charge for every download. You could also give it away and charge people to buy coins or tokens. People could pay money to upgrade their characters or buy into new worlds. The sky is the limit. I know you can do it.

Let your imagination run wild and write your ideas down because even if you don't make them happen now, you can always come back to them later.

REPAIRING DEVICES

Another way you can earn money is by learning how to fix computers, cell phones, tablets, or any other technology-related devices. Learning how to fix these gadgets can be a high-paying job or a side business for you to do for family and friends. This is also a skill you can learn by watching videos or reading books.

There also may be basic classes offered in your high school, which could build your foundation of how things work. You can then go on to more advanced courses once you graduate high school. You could attend a technical school specifically for fixing computers, or you could take classes at a local college.

If you think you can't afford it, you could look into getting grant money or other programs to help pay for it. Start looking into it now, so you're prepared for when you're ready. You can learn a lot of this by taking the time you spend on other things and redirecting it toward these new skills you want to learn.

FOCUS ON YOUR FUTURE

This chapter is full of constructive things you can do with your time. These are positive ways to distract you from any negativity you may have in your life. Choosing to do any of the things I just talked about can also take time away from things that will get you in trouble.

You can redirect your energy into hobbies, which can turn into skills and benefit you for years to come. By developing these positive habits of learning and being creative, you can feel good about knowing you're making progress toward becoming the best version of yourself.

Focus on your passions and what makes you happy. By becoming knowledgeable, you'll become confident. As long as what you're doing is not hurting anyone, go for it.

CHAPTER 15

MONEY — MAKE IT, SAVE IT, AND INVEST IT

The ways to make money are endless and more accessible than you may think. In this chapter, I will share with you not only ways to make money but also give you insight on how to manage it, save it, and invest it. I'll also talk about how it works to use other people's money in the form of credit.

I have already touched on some ways to make money with technology, getting a real estate license, and a few other methods throughout this book. Read on for even more ideas.

MAKE YOUR MONEY THE LEGAL WAY

Before you are tempted to break the law for money, stop and consider the consequences. You won't get away with stealing or any other form of illegal activity for very long. Everyone gets caught eventually. And when you do, I can assure you it will not be worth it. Between legal fees, fines, and losing your freedom, you will regret your actions. It will have lasting effects on the rest of your life. It's best to start legally and stay that way.

If you have done nothing wrong yet, keep it that way. It's important to know this information, so you're not persuaded when negative opportunities present themselves. There are more legitimate ways to make money than you could imagine. Based on my personal experience, when you work for something, you will appreciate it more.

DRIVING FOR MONEY

Having a driver's license offers you the freedom to travel, but it can also be valuable in helping you earn money. You could go a step further than a standard driver's license and get a commercial license, which would allow you to drive bigger vehicles. Tractor-trailer drivers often get paid extra to travel outside their local area. Becoming an over-the-road driver can have many benefits.

There are always jobs available for those with a commercial license. If this is something that interests you, there are schools that offer training and teach you how to get this type of license, and they often assist you in finding a job.

Having a driver's license will give you an advantage in getting just about any job. A noncommercial driver's license allows you to drive any vehicle under 26,000 pounds. These vehicles can include small box trucks, food delivery trucks, pickup trucks, or any car.

A few examples of things you can deliver are office supplies, furniture, flowers, and packages. You might want to deliver pizza like I did when I lived at the Jersey Shore. Search local businesses in your area to see which ones are looking to hire drivers. You could search the old-fashioned way and look in a local newspaper, or you could search online and find a job close to home. Look for something with flexible hours that will work with your schedule.

When you have a clean driving record, you can always find a job. If you do not own a car, sometimes you can drive the company's vehicle. Employers are always looking for a reliable person with a clean driving record. Having a license can give you more opportunities than you can imagine. Getting your driver's license is one of the smartest decisions you can make for yourself.

Another way you could earn income with a driver's license is to become an independent contractor. This type of work means you are your own boss and usually requires you to have a personal vehicle, but there are some exceptions.

When you have a job, you're considered a W2 employee. When you're an independent contractor, you become a sole proprietor for tax purposes, and you'll receive a 1099 tax form at the end of the year for the money you earned. As an independent contractor, you're able to write off your expenses, such as gas, tolls, car maintenance, mileage, and more. These expenses are deducted from your earned income and will reduce the amount of taxes you will have to pay.

Examples of independent contractor driving opportunities are rideshare services. Where you live and the time you're reading this book will determine the opportunities available to you. We're all familiar with the big ones, such as Uber and Lyft, but there are others. Some of these include food delivery services.

In most cases, they don't pay you by the hour. You get paid for the service you provide on an individual delivery basis. The company will take some fees, but in most cases, you can get paid almost instantly. I have worked with Uber and Lyft, accumulating five hundred rides between the two companies. I did this part-time for a couple of years while living in Florida.

Rideshare driving allowed me to get familiar with many of the beach towns and the theme park areas. I would turn off the app and explore places I found interesting between rides. It was nice to get paid to visit new locations, and I met a lot of interesting people from all around the world.

There are books you can buy to learn more about how to avoid some common mistakes made with rideshare driving. Do your research and ask questions of people that have experience with each company you are considering. If there are reviews about the company, you should always read them before making a final decision.

New companies are starting every day, so look to see what's available in your area. You can work with multiple companies at the same time. You don't need multiple phones; you can just switch between the apps. That is what I did, and it was not a problem. Just do your research first, as what I am telling you could change at any time.

GO THE EXTRA MILE

Whether you're working a job or operating your own business, do what needs to get done without someone having to tell you to do it. Going the extra mile means doing more than is expected of you. Work smart and hard at everything you do.

Being reliable and showing up on time makes you a valuable employee. Developing these habits early in life will ensure you have the foundation of a good quality work ethic. Dependability will set you apart from most other people. When something important needs to be accomplished, people will know they can count on you. Possessing these qualities is part of your character and will serve you well in other areas of your life too.

GETTING A JOB

When applying for a job, there are things you can do to increase your chances of getting hired. Once you have decided on the job you would like to apply for, do your research on the company and the position. Apply online or in-person, depending on which the company prefers. Be sure to provide accurate contact information so they will be able to get in touch with you. It's also a good idea to follow up with them and make sure your application was received. This follow-up will give you an opportunity to let them know you're excited and looking forward to hearing from them.

Some jobs require that you submit a resume, which is a history of your work experience, education, qualifications, skills, and references of people who can vouch for you. Your resume should be tailored to the type of work for which you are applying. You would, therefore, want to list previous jobs specifically related to that job application. There are many online resources to assist in the preparation of a resume. You can create one from scratch, or you can use a template. Always include a cover letter with your resume and consider having an adult help you if you're not sure how to do it.

When you go for a job interview, be on time for the appointment. Better yet, show up ten minutes early. Wear nice, clean clothes, have your hair combed, teeth brushed, and look well-rested. You will want to make a good first impression. Looking good and feeling good will give you the confidence, which employers can usually sense and is what they want in an employee.

Enthusiasm and a positive attitude will sometimes get you further than the actual skills required for the job. Most employers will be willing to train you on the specific skills needed. Explain that you are a self-starter, and you are coachable, teachable, and ready to learn. Often the most valuable skill you can have is to show a willingness to learn.

GETTING CREATIVE

If you're not old enough to get working papers, you'll need to be creative and learn how to hustle. You can do things from home, like making art or crafts or something else that you could sell locally. Are you good at painting or drawing? How about working with your hands, repurposing old things, and making them look new?

You could also wash cars, cut grass, babysit, or tutor someone in a subject at which you excel. Maybe you can make and sell jewelry. How about becoming a dog walker or a pet sitter?

Think about the ideas I gave you in the technology chapter. Have you thought of any small business owners who could use your technical experience? Have you considered becoming a social media influencer? If you think creatively, I'm sure you can come up with some ideas. Don't be afraid to ask someone for help.

EARNING MONEY WHILE YOU SLEEP

Much of my life, I worked in construction and odd jobs requiring physical labor. I was trading time for money on an hourly basis. When I was twenty-eight years old, I was introduced to a way of making money I never knew was possible for me. I think you deserve to be aware of it; I wish someone had taught me about it sooner. It's called residual income or royalties. These terms may not be familiar to you, but you see people on TV every day who make money this way. Residual income is when you do something one time, then get paid repeatedly. Popular examples of this are in the music and movie businesses.

When actors make a movie, they film it one time, then they get paid every time it's played in a theater, watched on TV, or purchased in any form. Musicians also make tons of money this way. They make the music one time, and they get paid every time a song is downloaded or played on the radio. In the movie and music businesses, this is known as royalties.

Authors of books also get paid royalties this way. They write the book one time and get paid a percentage every time someone buys it. If you write a good book now, it can earn money for you well into the future. The more books you write, the more money you can make.

The concept of doing something once and getting paid repeatedly fascinated me. I never imagined this was a way I could make money until someone showed me how.

I learned this concept in 2006 when I became an independent representative for a company in the telecommunications industry that offered a way to make residual income. Their latest product was a video phone. It used a high-speed internet connection and gave you the ability to see the person you were speaking with. This technology was relatively new back then. There were webcams and Skype, but this was different.

It was exciting to learn how I could sign up customers one time, and every month when they paid their bill, I would get a percentage. This was a game-changer for me. I never wanted to make money any other way after learning this method.

If this interests you, there are many companies in the home-based business industry. Typically, getting started only has two basic requirements; you must be eighteen years old and be willing to pay a small startup fee to join most companies. If you can get excited about the product or service they offer, you'll have a better chance of success.

Do your research and make sure the company is legitimate before you give them any personal information or money. You can read some reviews and check with the Better Business Bureau to see what their rating is before making any commitment.

After a couple of years with this company, I discovered other industries that offered this way of earning an income. It was amazing how many opportunities there were for ordinary people like me to make money this way. This new-found knowledge led me to discovering how to make money on the Internet. I became obsessed with finding new ways to use technology to create an income and get me out of doing physical labor for money.

INTERNET MARKETING

This section is about using the internet to create multiple streams of residual income. Internet marketing, affiliate marketing, and ways to use the Internet to make money are something anyone can learn how to do. You can look at some of my old YouTube videos to see what I was doing when I first got started.

Affiliate marketing was a concept that blew my mind. We all refer things to people every day, but we don't usually get paid for it. Have you told someone about a good movie you saw recently? When they went to the theater to see it, did you make any money? If you were an affiliate of the movie theater, you would have earned a commission.

When I built a website for someone who was going to use it to sell something, they usually needed several systems to make it work. I would then refer these necessary monthly services to my customers. Every month, when they paid the bill for those services, I received a small commission. It didn't cost them any more money, and I got a referral fee from the companies whose services I shared.

This concept of affiliate marketing is still something I use today. When you understand how it works, you can use it as streams of income for yourself. Go to the bottom of any major website and look for a link to its affiliate program. Sign up for a free account. Once you are approved, you will receive personalized links you can share.

You can email your links to friends and family, or set up a website where you can promote all your affiliate products in one place. If you are under the age of eighteen, you may need an adult to set up these accounts. If you don't have an adult to do this for you, learn as much about this concept as you can until you are old enough to do it for yourself. There is a lot to know about this topic, and you are never too young to start learning.

MANAGING MONEY

When you have money, you must be smart about how you spend it. This also includes your parent's money. Try not to waste money on things you don't need. If you make a habit of being careful about what you spend your money on now, you will have a lot more when you need it later.

If you intend to get your own place to live or buy a car one day, it will require that you save money. Save now, so you have a sizeable amount when that time comes. I briefly mentioned earlier in this book how expensive it can be to live on your own. Another significant expense will be buying a car.

I know it's tempting to buy expensive shoes or clothes, but it's often unnecessary. It's not wise to overspend on clothing you will ruin, outgrow, or only wear once a year. Don't get caught up in paying extra for name brands. Get something that looks nice at a reasonable price and put the extra money in the bank.

If you spend every dollar you get, it will be impossible for you to have savings to fall back on in case of an emergency. It's okay to treat yourself occasionally, but don't let money burn a hole in your pocket. Just because you have money doesn't mean you need to spend it.

Consider going food shopping and eating at home instead of eating out all the time. This choice is an important decision you can make when managing your money. Realize how much things cost when making a purchase and shop around for lower prices when possible. If you're in a store and an item seems expensive, pull out your phone and see if you can get a better price online. It may take an extra day to get it, but you could save money.

Keep track of what you spend, and you will start to realize how much money you waste. If money is scarce, the last thing you should do is waste it when you have it. Don't think of this way of living as being cheap; just consider yourself as being a smart, thrifty person.

SAVING MONEY

The most effective way to save money is to have a bank account. If you're under the age of eighteen, you'll need an adult to cosign for you. Find someone you can trust and open a checking account and a savings account. Then open your own accounts when you're old enough to do so.

The checking account will be for everyday purchases and will have a debit card attached to it. You should use this for daily purchases, like food and the basics you need to get by. You'll also use this account to pay your bills, which you'll have when you're on your own.

Your savings account is where you put the money you don't touch unless there is an emergency. Put extra money you don't need for daily living expenses into this account. Saving your money this way is how you will have enough money to buy a car and move into your own apartment or house when the time comes. Putting as much as you can in savings now will ensure you are prepared to make big purchases later.

When you have a job, your paycheck can be deposited directly into your bank accounts. Be sure to have a percentage of your paycheck deposited into your savings, as well as your checking account. If your employer pays you in cash, put it in the bank right away before you find a way to spend it. Do not keep a lot of cash out unless you need it for something specific. When the money is in the bank, it's easier to forget about it. Using this advice as a guide will help you get in the habit of saving money.

There's an old saying, *out of sight, out of mind*. Anytime you get a sizeable sum of money, you should put at least half in your savings account. Birthday money can be an excellent opportunity to build up your savings. Remember, your spending money will be in your checking account.

Use the strategies I mentioned in the managing section. When you get a discount on something expensive, deposit the money you saved in the bank. It was money you were willing to spend anyway, and you won't miss it. As you get into the habit of saving, it will become easier as time goes on. Challenge yourself to save a certain amount of money by a specific date. This goal will motivate you to get creative and find ways to earn more money. Don't forget, keep it legal!

INVESTING YOUR TIME AND MONEY

It's useful for you to understand the concept of investing. You can start by purchasing something inexpensive, find a way to increase its value, and sell it for more than you paid for it. Finding ways to make your money grow are all around you. Let me give you an example of how this can work for you.

Let's say you go to a yard sale and they are selling a bicycle for twenty dollars. It's a good quality bike, but it has a flat tire and a rusty frame. You can buy it, fix the flat tire, sand down the rust and use a can of spray paint to give it a fresh look. Then you can resell the bike to someone for fifty dollars and make a profit of thirty dollars minus the couple bucks you spent on a patch kit and spray paint—this is a small investment of money and a little bit of your time.

Now you can take this profit and reinvest it into something else. This is just an example of something you can do right now, to take the money you're earning from the odd jobs you're doing and making it grow.

I want to help you recognize the opportunities that are all around you. Have you ever seen a nice piece of furniture in someone's trash? What if you took it home, cleaned it up, and painted it, then sold it for one hundred dollars? Doing this wouldn't require much money and would be a good investment of your time. You could do this all week and then have a yard sale of your own on the weekend. When you start to think creatively, you will be amazed at what you can do.

You can also have long term investment strategies. Start learning how the stock market works so you can understand how to buy stocks in publicly traded companies. You can start with a custodial account if you are under eighteen years old. It will require an adult to be on the account with you. Once you're eighteen, their name will be removed. You can invest from your computer with an account through an online broker.

I have learned the basics of online trading in the last few years, but I wish I had started earlier in life. Online Trading is not something you'll learn about in high school, so do your own research. Small investments like this can earn you big profits over the next five to ten years. This is an example of how you get your money to work for you while you're out doing other things to make more money. Having different investments are how you create multiple streams of income.

You can also learn how to invest in real estate. People buy houses to live in, but they are also a good investment. When the value increases, they can be sold for a profit. This profit can sometimes be significant and used as a down payment to buy another house.

People also buy houses and rent them out to someone who pays a monthly payment. This is called being a landlord and can be very profitable. Many people make a living through rental income. There are also ways to buy cheap houses that need work, invest in fixing them up, and sell them for a profit. Real estate can be a good investment if you know what you're doing, but you can lose money if you're not knowledgeable.

There are many ways to invest money and something you can learn more about with a little bit of research. You can get books from the library to learn the details of how these different investing methods work. The things I have mentioned here are only the tip of the iceberg.

Making money is easy, even if you don't think so right now. You can learn and understand more about money by reading books and magazines on the topic. You can see how rich people have made their money and find out how they invested it to make their money grow.

Once you have some money, you can invest it and have your money work for you. There is no age requirement for learning about money. The more prepared you are now, the better off you will be as an adult armed with all the knowledge you gain. The best investment I have ever made has been in developing myself. Investing in yourself will be one of the most rewarding things you ever do.

UNDERSTANDING CREDIT

Having good credit will allow you to borrow money from banks and other private lenders and pay it back with monthly payments. Using credit is how most people buy real estate. They use their good credit to get a mortgage loan. It's also the way you can walk into a car dealership and buy a car with no money down. If you have good credit, it can be more valuable than cash in some cases. Credit is also essential in getting approved for a credit card, which gives you the ability to make a purchase today and pay for it later.

Your credit is based on a score ranging from 300 on the low end to 850 on the high end. If you have an 850, you have the best credit possible. This is a very hard thing to achieve, but you don't need your score to be that high to have good credit. Anywhere around 700 is usually good enough to get approved for most loans. The higher your score, the lower the interest rate you'll pay on a loan. If your score is too low, you may need to get someone with better credit to co-sign for you when applying for a loan.

You can build your credit by paying your bills on time. Consider having your cell phone account in your own name to help you build credit now. Keeping your credit card balances low will also help your credit score. Paying the balance in full is best and will help you avoid paying interest.

Building good credit is a topic you can learn much more about on your own. I just want to give you the basics and make you aware of what credit is and why it is important. It is essential to make smart decisions when using your credit. It can take years to build up good credit, but one poor decision can ruin it for you in an instant.

SELF-EDUCATION

These are all things I learned through self-education and personal experience. I wanted to share this financial information with you because I believe you deserve more of a financial education than a basic math class has to offer. I'm sure this will be helpful to you.

Yes, you can learn some of this through college, but it's more valuable to learn it on your own now to avoid making mistakes early on in life. You can take courses, buy books, watch videos, and research any of these topics right now at any age. For you to become the smartest version of yourself, you will need to take the initiative and become your own teacher. Stay in school and learn as much as you can, but never stop educating yourself with specialized knowledge.

In the next and final chapter, I will talk about more of the personal development and self-help strategies I have used to change my entire life for the better. I have spent tens of thousands of dollars and the last fourteen years of my life learning this information. I am about to give you the cliff notes' version of everything that has worked for me, and what I know can work for you.

CHAPTER 16

SELF-DEVELOPMENT STRATEGIES

I n this chapter, I will tie together all the individual personal development topics I've covered throughout this book with the addition of more strategies you can use to improve the quality of your life. The single best investment I have ever made has been into myself by improving my self-worth utilizing this information and practicing the disciplines I am sharing with you.

Some of the most successful people in the world give credit to self-help books and seminars for creating the happiness and wealth they have in their lives. These strategies, combined with my personal experiences, are giving you a unique view of what you can do to create the life of your dreams. Apply what you're learning, and you will be amazed at the results you achieve.

I believe you deserve to have the same opportunities as the most accomplished people in the world. I wish someone would have shared this with me when I was younger. I know it could have changed the path I took. Now I hope you will use it to change yours.

MINDSET

Changing the way you choose to live your life starts in your mind. If your life is not working the way you want it to, consider making some changes. Changing your habits will require a shift in the way you think. If you apply self-discipline and commit to implementing these new strategies for one year, I can assure you, your life will never be the same.

Committing to long-term personal development will improve the quality of your life. You will become a more valuable person to yourself and the world around you. If you have the desire, it's a decision you can make today—no more excuses and no more blaming other people. Take responsibility for the results you have in your life. You are important. Love yourself.

Your self-image is attached to your belief system. If you think you're good looking and smart, you'll see yourself that way. If you think negative thoughts about yourself, you may start to believe them. When you change the way you see yourself, the way other people see you will also change. Become confident in who you are as a person. Create a vision of what your new self-image looks like and work towards becoming that version of yourself.

Once you believe in yourself, have self-confidence, and develop your self-esteem, any thoughts of other people being better than you or more deserving than you will vanish. Stop focusing on your past, live in the moment, and look toward the future. Decide what you want out of life and make it your mission to accomplish it. Develop a vision for your future, and think about how you want it to look, then commit to finding a way to make it happen.

A powerful tool you can use is called a vision board. You cut out pictures from magazines of the things you want to have in your life. Then you glue them to a poster board and hang it where you will see it every day. You can have pictures of the house you want to live in, the car you want to own, images of places you want to visit, and anything else you want in your future. When you look at this board, believe you will have these things in your life one day.

Once you know what it is you want, commit to working towards achieving it. Commitment is doing what you said you would do, after the mood you said it in has worn off. Being committed is directly related to persistence, which I will talk about shortly. When you're applying all these things together, you're increasing your odds of living a fulfilled life.

Don't let other people discourage your dreams. When you have big ideas, be prepared for obstacles. If you get knocked down, get back up. You determine what defeat looks like to you. Suppose you become discouraged, read about the lives of people who overcame significant obstacles to achieve their dreams, and have changed the world. Don't let rejection freeze you in your tracks.

UNDERSTANDING YOUR "WHY"

Once you find your purpose in life and become clear on what you are meant to do, knowing why you're doing it will motivate you to keep going when times get tough. Is there something you've been thinking about for years but haven't taken the actions needed to get it done? If the same idea continues to pop into your mind, this could have something to do with your purpose.

For example, if you feel your mission in life is to help other people, you should align your thoughts and actions toward that effort. There are many ways you can accomplish this. You could help the homeless by volunteering at a local soup kitchen or shelter. You might consider starting a charity that would raise money for the specific type of people you want to help. Or, maybe your focus could be on helping babies who are in need.

People's "whys" are often related to personal experience because that's what has real meaning for them. For example, if someone has battled a specific illness, they start a charity to raise awareness and money to find a cure for that illness. Have you had a personal experience that could motivate you to help others? When your "why" is big enough, it will become the driving force for accomplishing your goals.

Because of how I grew up, my "why" for writing this book is to help at-risk teenagers avoid feeling helpless like I did. I want you to know how to raise yourself if necessary. I want you to have the knowledge you need to take charge of your life. I want to share my knowledge and experience so you can avoid all the mistakes I made.

Growing up in unfortunate circumstances shouldn't hold you back from achieving your dreams. I am on a mission to teach you everything I can to help level the playing field for you. As uncomfortable as it can be to put myself out here like this, I believe it is my purpose to do so. If I can help you avoid going down the wrong path, you'll be helping me achieve one of my goals.

SETTING GOALS

Most people don't set goals because they may be told repeatedly that they can't do something, so they start to believe it's not possible. Then, because of a poor self-image and a lack of self-esteem, they don't think they deserve to have the result of their goal. Don't let this type of conditioning hold you back from setting goals for yourself. When you set a goal, always believe you'll achieve it and that you deserve it. Set goals that are realistic and achievable to avoid becoming discouraged.

Goals work for everyone who sets them and takes the necessary action steps to achieve the results. Identify the goal, why you want to achieve it, and the date you will attain it by. You don't always need an exact plan to get started; you just need the desire. Your goals will create actions, which will create motivation. The more you focus on the goal, the ideas of how to accomplish it will start coming to you.

You already set goals without realizing it. If you have a plan to watch a movie tonight, that's a goal. You already know how to do it. Commit to doing something every day to help move you closer to achieving the results you desire. Keep the reason you're doing something fresh in your mind; this will help motivate you and give you a sense of purpose as you're working toward your goals.

When you want to accomplish a specific goal, writing it down on paper helps make your goals real. Post them somewhere you can see them every day. You should set goals for all things you want to accomplish, big or small. Your list will always be evolving into bigger and better things. Once you achieve a goal on your list, check it off, and then add something new. It's really a great feeling of accomplishment to be able to check a goal off your list.

You should have short-term goals, mid-range goals, and long-term goals. These are daily, weekly, monthly, yearly, five- and ten-year goals. Be willing to make small sacrifices now, to enjoy greater rewards in the future. Having self-discipline is the key to avoiding temptations.

Having goals is essential since you can't hit a target you can't see. Once you start to focus on accomplishing something, your subconscious mind will go to work on helping you accomplish it. Write out your goals and the steps you need to take to achieve them. Break each goal into small manageable chunks. Your goals should be specific, measurable, achievable, and realistic.

Look at your goals every day to keep them fresh in your mind. Remembering why you're working towards achieving your goals will help you overcome procrastination. You can find an account-ability partner to help keep you on track. Find a way to reward yourself each time you achieve a goal. You should have different goals for every area of your life. Setting goals is only the first step. If you seriously want to accomplish them, you must be persistent.

PERSISTENCE

Too many people quit before they reach their goals. Your per-sistence is what will keep you going when obstacles get in your way. When you make it your mission to accomplish something, persistence will give you the strength to overcome any challenge you have to face to achieve your goal. Having a strong "why" and purposeful intent will fuel your persistence.

If you need examples of persistence in action, read the story of Thomas Edison and how many tries it took him to find a way to create the lightbulb before eventually succeeding. Look up the story of Walt Disney, and how many times he was denied the financing he needed to build his dream theme park before achieving his goal. They never quit trying to accomplish these seemingly impossible tasks. Anything is possible when you make a commitment and never give up.

SELF-DOUBT

If you are always second-guessing yourself with every little decision you make, it will affect your self-confidence. Doubting yourself usually happens when you don't have enough knowledge of a situation, so learn all you can about whatever it is you're trying to accomplish. The more educated you become, the more confident you will be. Don't let other people discourage you from what you know you are capable of doing.

If you doubt how well you play a particular sport, take lessons to get better. Whenever you struggle with a subject in life, do everything you can to learn more about it. As you become more knowledgeable, the doubt will fade away. You can be confident in knowing you're doing everything possible to improve yourself on any topic or project.

Don't be so hard on yourself when you struggle at something. The way we learn, as humans, is through personal experience. When you don't do something the way you wanted to, learn from your mistakes, and make improvements. Being hard on yourself up because you made a wrong decision will only discourage you more. Never put yourself down. Encourage yourself by always believing you're doing the best you can. Through education and practice, you can become good at anything. Believe in yourself!

AFFIRMATIONS

Affirming what you want in your life is a powerful way of making it happen. Writing down what you want to accomplish and then saying it out loud builds your belief that it can happen. You can create affirmations for any of your goals. Doing this helps to make them real and embeds them into your subconscious mind. Repeating affirmations of the things you want to accomplish most creates a stronger belief that you will achieve the goals you set for yourself.

For example, if you are working towards becoming healthier, you may say, *I am becoming healthier every day through my healthy eating habits and my exercise routine.* Reciting this to yourself will reassure that you are moving in a positive direction toward achieving this goal.

Other things you might consider affirming out loud are, *I'm learning from my mistakes. I'm becoming smarter every day. I know I can achieve any goal I set for myself. I love myself. I am becoming a better friend. I am becoming a happier person. I am becoming more self-confident with every day that passes.*

Be careful not to say negative affirmations accidentally. If you're singing along to songs with negative lyrics, you could be memorizing and repeating self-sabotaging language. There are positive and negative affirmations. Whatever it is you repeat to yourself consistently is reaffirming that thought to your subconscious mind.

If you put positive information into your mind, you'll become a more positive person. If you're putting negative information into your mind, you're hindering your ability to improve yourself. If you read inspirational books, you'll become inspired. If you read hateful books, you will be filling your mind with hateful thoughts. You can control what you put into your mind, so always focus on feeding it positive knowledge.

POSITIVE THINKING

Thinking positive is how you become optimistic. By focusing on the positive in life, you'll attract positive things to you. If you're always thinking positive, you'll have a better chance of succeeding at whatever you do. It can change your entire outlook on life. Surround yourself with optimistic people, and it will rub off onto you.

Changing your ways and your behaviors may not come naturally. You've been conditioned to think and behave a certain way. You may need to deprogram your mind to reprogram it with more positive thinking. Just like when you want to install a new program on your computer, you must uninstall the old program first. It works the same way for your brain. You may resist these changes at first but commit to staying the course.

If reading books on how to become better at something is new to you, be patient, and incorporate them into your lifestyle gradually. Once you start to do this consistently, it will become a habit and will seem natural. Your brain is a powerful computer. Instead of only reading books to be entertained, gradually add in some on helping you learn how to become better in a specific area of your life. Reading, watching, and listening to positive and inspirational information will naturally begin to change the way you think.

If you keep doing the same things you've always done, you'll continue getting the same results. If you're unhappy with a specific aspect of your life, focus on finding ways to change your thoughts and habits around that area. You'll need to work harder on yourself than you do on any job. Working to become a more valuable person can be challenging. Consistency is the key. Just focus on getting a little bit better every day.

A small amount of exercise and a little bit of reading something positive every day will turn into positive habits. Try doing this in the morning to jump-start your day. Eventually, you can increase the amount of time you spend doing these activities.

You may begin with fifteen minutes of reading an inspirational book and then increase it to thirty minutes after a month. Once you start to enjoy it, you may want to read for an hour each day. Instead of listening to music on your morning commute, listen to a motivational or educational podcast. These small changes can make a big difference.

Always being positive will enhance your mental attitude. When you're positive and optimistic about your situation, you'll become a happier person. An example of thinking positive is if you have a big test coming up, study diligently, and expect you'll get a good grade. Be confident that you're well prepared. If you focus on getting a bad grade or failing the test, you will attract failing results.

If you talk to a friend on the phone who is always positive, it will begin to rub off on you. Being a positive person is contagious. When you're always upbeat and happy, you'll notice that others around you will be too. Being negative is also contagious, so try to avoid negative people. Spending time with a negative person can discourage your positive spirit.

Becoming a positive person is a choice. Having a positive attitude will attract powerful results in your life. Set your goals and believe you will achieve them. Share your optimism with others. Helping others feel better about themselves will make you feel better too.

PASSION

We are all passionate about something in our lives. Is your passion benefiting you or only occupying your time? Is it for entertainment, or is it helping you move toward your life's big goals? Sometimes we get caught up in the excitement of things that don't serve our greater good. We become passionate about the wrong things.

I've been a victim of this behavior. I had slowly become so passionate about entertaining myself that I neglected my mind and body in the process. If you want to live a long and prosperous life, you need to make important decisions about how you spend your time. Understand, time is more valuable than money. You can always make more money, but you can't ever get more time. Learn the value of time management and become good at it.

If you're doing something for the right reason, have faith, and go after it with good intentions. Believe things will work out in your favor. Your friends may not initially understand the changes you're making but be enthusiastic about your ideas and desires. Your enthusiasm and excitement are what will sell your vision to the people around you.

Control your enthusiasm and direct your energy into a passion with a purpose. You can change what you're passionate about at any time. It may not happen overnight, but you can do it over time. Once you identify your new, positive passion, gradually cut back on the old stuff and add time to the new things you want to do.

For me, I redirected my passion for going to football games, which consumed an entire day and began watching the games on TV with my family, which only requires three hours of my time. I stopped going to motorcycle rallies and concerts, and now I have more time to take family vacations. In addition to having more quality time with my wife and stepdaughter, reducing the time I spent being passionate about these hobbies gave me more time to develop new passions.

The idea of writing a book like this has been on my mind for many years, but I was too busy to gain the momentum I needed to get it done. I still like doing those other things, but I'm much less passionate about them now. With the time I saved by staying at home, I slowly started to learn how to write and publish this book. Because I have shifted my focus and passion, you are now able to read this finished product.

Once I took the first step towards becoming a writer, I began to get excited about the possibilities. This new passion has led me to create other ways of sharing my knowledge and experiences. I created a podcast, I started my own self-help company, and I'm looking forward to getting back into public speaking. The process of writing this book has also reignited my passion for creating websites and inspirational videos.

I have realized my purpose in life and have made the necessary changes to accommodate how to make it happen. None of this was possible when I was too busy cruising around the country on my Harley or regularly attending concerts and sporting events. I made this decision a couple of years ago, but because I had so much to learn, it took longer than expected. I had to overcome many obstacles, but I never lost focus of finding a way to share this information with you.

Develop a passion for whatever it is you want to do with your life. Try to find a balance between fun and profit. Moderation is the key. Don't become so immersed in one thing that you forget about everything else. If you know you want to do something but at first you don't succeed, learn more about it and try again.

Become persistent and make it your mission to achieve your dreams. When you decide what it is you want, work hard, and focus on becoming better at it. Make the necessary sacrifices. Don't be afraid to try new things. You'll develop a passion for something once you understand it more and get excited about it.

KNOWLEDGE IS THE KEY

Traditional education will give you an essential foundation in subjects like reading, math, English, science, social studies, and history, which are all extremely valuable. Self-education will help you learn more specific skills. The journey of teaching yourself can last a lifetime. When you want to know more about any particular skill or talent, take the time to look it up and study it. Knowledge is power. How much power do you want?

If you want to have expensive things in life—a big house, beautiful cars, lots of money, and an above-average life—it won't come easy. Focus on educating yourself as much as possible now so that you can have all those expensive items later. Now is the time to resist instant pleasures and make sacrifices to benefit the bigger picture of your life. Develop your self-discipline, be willing to work hard, and avoid the get rich quick schemes.

Make a list of ideas based on the topics in this book that interested you most. Get your library card and start taking out books on those topics. These will likely lead you to other related subjects. Start researching topics online, watch videos about them, and explore your creativity. As you start to research things, you'll gravitate toward one or two subjects. Once you know what it is you like, you can dive deeper into learning more about those topics. Follow your passions.

MENTORS AND COACHES

I don't expect you to do all of these things I've talked about on your own. I recommend you find someone or a group of people who are willing to support and encourage you along this journey. Find a mentor or a coach. These are people who have experience and knowledge about what you're trying to accomplish. A coach will help you become better at whatever it is your doing, and a mentor will help guide you there.

Regardless of what your focus, there's someone out there who can assist you. It can be your guidance counselor, the coach of a school sport, or a parent or family member who makes you feel comfortable. People care about you more than you may think. When adults see a young person, who is serious about improving themselves, they're usually willing to help any way they can.

When someone knows you are truly committed, he or she will want to help you even more. There will be people who may feel the need to test you first to make sure you are serious. Pass the test and accept their help. Making significant changes in your life will require some support. Don't try and go at it all alone every time. There is power in teamwork. Even if it's just someone to bounce your ideas off of, find someone you can trust.

Not all of your mentors and coaches will be people you see in person. When I started my self-improvement journey, I was being mentored by books and audio programs from people I had never met. When I found someone whose teaching style resonated with me, I purchased their other books, watched them in videos, listened to them on audio, and attended their seminars. They didn't know they were my mentor, but for me, it was like I was the only one they were talking to when I was listening to or reading their stuff.

With technology today, it's easier than ever to follow the people who you can relate to and enjoy their style of teaching. I would love to be the one who mentors and coaches you to the next level of your life. I plan to continue creating new content you can use to develop the areas of your life I have talked about in this book. I also plan to blog, podcast, and do live streaming videos about these topics and related subjects that didn't make it into the book. If you are following me on social media and subscribed to my email list, you will always be up to date on what I am doing.

KEEPING A JOURNAL

Document the problems you encounter and how you solved them. You want to avoid making the same mistakes twice. Writing things on paper will help them become clear. Often when writing out a problem, you can come up with the answer. Problem solving is not just for math; it also applies to life's challenges. Keeping this information in a journal will give you the ability to reflect on it in the future.

Capture good ideas. If you don't write them down, they could be lost forever. Don't rely only on your memory. You may not act on these ideas right away, but they will be there for a later date when you need them. It may be years before you use the ideas you wrote down, but you can always add to an idea or merge it with others to create a better one.

Your journal is a filing system for your thoughts and ideas. You can use it to make notes or document highlights from books you've read or conversations you've had. You can use it to write out and keep track of your goals. Always keep it with you when possible. You never know when inspiration will strike.

You could describe your feelings about the good and bad days you experience. Write without restrictions, and don't worry about punctuation. Draw pictures or cut out articles from the newspaper. There are no rules in your journal, but it's helpful to put the date, time, and location of the entry. Talk to yourself through your journal by writing about interesting things you see and do throughout your day.

By documenting all these things, you're writing a version of your life story. You will begin to see patterns in your life. You will notice changes in yourself. You will become better with your communication skills, and it will become easier to express yourself.

If you write down how things are for you, it could help to better understand what someone else may be going through. Writing things down when they happen will help you remember all the little details you would most likely forget later.

Discipline yourself to use it regularly. You could start by writing about how things are for you right now. Tell it like it is, with no filter. For example, you can write down what you like or don't like about this book. Write down all the results of your research on the money-making topics, or document what skill you might want to develop from the technology chapter.

Write a list of places you want to travel to in your life. Make a list of your ideal jobs or businesses you want to start. Write out the action plans for accomplishing your goals. Become the author of your own life and consider writing a legacy your children will be able to read about someday.

Keeping a journal may be awkward for you at first, but it will be helpful in understanding who you are as a person. You don't need to write every thought or feeling, just the most important things you don't want to forget.

You can just keep a positive journal if you choose. Start by writing down all the positive things you have in your life. Write down things you are grateful for. If you had a good experience with an adult in your life, or maybe you had a day with no fighting or negativity, write it down. These are things worth documenting. If you feel you always have bad days, every good day is worth writing down. Reread your journals every so often.

If you are bad at remembering names and you meet a person you don't want to forget, write their name down. Write who they were, where you met the person, and if they complimented you. When someone compliments you, write it down. Then when you are having a bad day, you can go back and read all the positive things people have said about you.

It's the little wins in life that will help uplift you on bad days. You may not get appreciation from people every day, so when you do, treasure it by writing it down so you can use it to boost your spirits later. A journal can be an essential tool in improving your life.

Start by getting a writing book. It doesn't have to be anything fancy. A simple notebook will do. Get into the habit of writing something every day. Start by writing a couple of words. You can start by saying something as simple as, *Today I ate meatloaf, and it was disgusting. I am never eating it again.*

Tomorrow you may add a few more words. Just one sentence will get you started, and then you can grow from there. Take baby steps; no need to overdo it at first. There are many ways a journal can be a benefit to you. Success leaves clues, and almost all successful people keep a journal.

I'M PROUD OF YOU

If you employ this information, it will help keep you out of trouble and ensure you have a better chance of success at anything you do. Applying the things I talked about in this book will improve the quality of your life in many ways. Where you are now will determine which areas you want to focus on first. Implement as much of this information as relates to you.

Take action and become excited about your future. You can become much more than you are right now. You are young, and you have so much room to grow. Your future is bright. Believe in yourself, set your goals, and work hard to achieve them. Commit to becoming a better person, and the world around you will become better.

Congratulations on finishing this book! Good luck in achieving everything you set your mind to and reach out to me if I can help in any way. I'm looking forward to hearing about your success story!

Ben Corlow

THANK YOU

Thank you for purchasing and reading this book. Writing and publishing this book has been a dream of mine for years. It has changed my life by writing it, and I hope it changes your life by reading it. If you apply the information from this book to your life, you will be amazed at how it can transform you. I look forward to hearing about the results you achieve.

I would love to hear your testimonial and get your feedback on how this book has helped you. Please review this book on the website from which you purchased it. If it was a gift, reach out to the person who gave it to you, thank them, and let them know what you thought of this information, and please ask them to leave the review for you. Please tell your friends about this book and share it on social media. Thank you.

To assist you in continuing your personal development, I would like to give you four of the most influential self-help books ever written for free. Go to my company website and join my email list for access to these free ebooks.

There are additional resources related to the topics in the book on my website. I will continue adding new information to assist you in learning more about the individual subjects in this book and other related material. Once you're on my email list, you will be easily updated as new information is created, including future books, social media pages, blogs, podcasts, videos, live streaming video events, and more. Visit www.TheSelfHelpCompany.com

ABOUT THE AUTHOR

Ben Povlow was born in Philadelphia, PA, in 1977. After growing up as an at-risk youth, while still a young adult, he continued to struggle to break free of his negative environment. He wanted a better life but didn't know how to achieve it. When he was twenty-eight years old, he became aware of self-help and personal development materials that would transform him in a way he never knew was possible.

He went on to improve the quality of his life by reading books, listening to audio trainings, and going to seminars of the most recognizable names in self-improvement. He followed these leaders around the country for several years, soaking up their knowledge and investing a lot of money into learning how to become the best version of himself he could be.

Ben believes we all have the power to change our circumstances through the way we think, act, and see ourselves. He has overcome many obstacles in his life and believes that if he can do it, anyone can.

He is now living the life of his dreams. He is married and lives with his wife, Kathi, and stepdaughter, Katelyn, in a quiet suburb in central North Carolina. Ben has committed himself to improve the lives of others by sharing his knowledge and experience. He is an inspiring motivational public speaker, a certified life coach, author, and business owner. You can learn more about Ben, his company, and services by visiting www.TheSelfHelpCompany.com

CPSIA information can be obtained
at www.ICGtesting.com
Printed in the USA
BVHW041304120221
600004BV00015B/266